Make Something
Good Today

summer 2013

MAKE SOMETHING GOOD TODAY

a memoir

ERIN & BEN NAPIER

G

GALLERY BOOKS

NEW YORK   LONDON   TORONTO   SYDNEY   NEW DELHI

Gallery Books
An Imprint of Simon & Schuster, Inc.
1230 Avenue of the Americas
New York, NY 10020

First Gallery Books hardcover edition October 2018

GALLERY BOOKS and colophon are registered trademarks of Simon & Schuster, Inc.

For information about special discounts for bulk purchases,
please contact Simon & Schuster Special Sales at 1-866-506-1949
or business@simonandschuster.com.

The Simon & Schuster Speakers Bureau can bring authors
to your live event. For more information or to book an event,
contact the Simon & Schuster Speakers Bureau at 1-866-248-3049
or visit our website at www.simonspeakers.com.

Jacket and interior page design by Erin Napier
Front jacket photograph by Beth Morgan
Back jacket photograph by Erin Napier
Jacket and title-page hand lettering by Novia Jonatan
Illustrations by Erin Napier

Unless noted otherwise, photos are from the authors' personal collection.

Song lyrics appearing on page 78 are from "Shiftwork," by Kenny Chesney.

Manufactured in the United States of America

1   3   5   7   9   10   8   6   4   2

Library of Congress Cataloging-in-Publication Data

Names: Napier, Erin, author. | Napier, Ben, author.
Title: Make something good today / by Erin and Ben Napier.
Description: First Gallery Books hardcover edition.
New York : Gallery Books, 2018.
Identifiers: LCCN 2018017981 (print) | LCCN 2018021239 (ebook)
ISBN 9781501189128 (ebook) | ISBN 9781501189111 (hardback)
ISBN 9781501189388 (trade paperback)
Subjects: LCSH: Napier, Erin. | Napier, Ben.
Television personalities—United States—Biography.
BISAC: BIOGRAPHY & AUTOBIOGRAPHY / Personal Memoirs.
Classification: LCC PN1992.4.N26 (ebook) | LCC PN1992.4.N26 A3 2018 (print)
DDC 791.4502/8092 [B]—dc23
LC record available at https://lccn.loc.gov/2018017981

ISBN 978-1-5011-8911-1
ISBN 978-1-5011-8912-8 (ebook)

For Helen,
our best production

Contents

Preface

Erin

It's so quiet I can hear Ben's Sunday watch ticking on the nightstand. I can't even remember the last time I had time to be here at home alone, piddling. The circus has dispersed, the loud whirlwind of production has vanished, and the film crew who became our patchwork family has gone home. The residue of chaos and noise remains, but the house is entirely silent.

Maybe when people think of what it's like making a TV show, they imagine air-conditioned trailers, hair and makeup people, and a team of personal assistants. The reality of our show is that you bring what you need to set and if you forget something, you run home and find it. We get up before dawn, exercise so the camera doesn't make us look as though we just woke up, and walk the dogs. Then we grab Ben's thermos of iced coffee and my gargantuan set bag, which Ben throws over his shoulder, and head out to whichever of three to five houses we're working on that morning.

We spend our days working in a heat so consuming it is hard to breathe in some of the more dilapidated houses. Some have cracked windows with vines growing into the room, right through the crown molding. Some have the acrid smell of bat infestation. And all of them leave salty, sweaty grit on our skin: to achieve perfect sound quality during shooting, no fans are allowed on. It's very glamorous.

My makeup bag, bigger and heavier than a regular one, carries all the tricks to make me look nor-mal in 100-degree heat. It holds a jar of crunchy peanut butter and a bag of plastic spoons, because everyone else on set likes creamy. There is a hand-held fan with batteries that are dead from the fan's being accidentally left on in transit. Cheap hair-spray, my only hope against Mississippi humidity. Bug spray, for the early days of the renovations in soggy, rotten houses where swarms of fleas and mosquitoes search for dinner.

All that has just slipped away. Now I remember it only as an extraordinary adventure we were privileged to be part of—an exhausting and invig-orating kind of grown-up summer camp.

There's a reason we love transforming a house from an old, decrepit, sometimes crumbling mess into a warm, inviting, revitalized home. It's a moving experience getting to watch a second life start to take shape. It's a history and a future uniting in one delicious moment. And we are in a place where we belong. Where we feel safe and loved and, hope-fully, inspired.

Our love of the process has nothing to do with new sofas, fresh paint, or artisan tile. Those are only the tools. The details. It's really about the mo-ment of the reveal: the tears we feel in our throats when the new homeowners stare wide-eyed at the home they never thought was possible. The one they had imagined come to life. The whole thing is personal. And that's the point.

That sense of wonder, that ability to hope for the impossible, is inside all of us. It is how we were created to be: always changing, always evolving. These qualities are built into us. The home becomes the hopeful symbol, the arrow pointing forward. It can support a person, solidify a relationship, or bring a small town that's lost its legs back to life.

Our lives are not so different from these homes. It all starts with our foundations, the things that drive us and make our hearts beat a little faster. The things we believe in and cherish—our families, our dearest friends, our faith—those are our bedrock. If they are sturdy—"square and plumb," as my mama says—we can weather any storm. They are built to last. We are built to last.

We build on a foundation, and soon it begins to look like more than just a slab; it's the bones of the life we always wanted: the dream.

The houses we rehabilitate begin as victims of time and circumstance, weeds and water damage, bad renovations patched together with particleboard, true craftsmanship buried under trends and fads that have vanished into the air like the thin ideas they once were. We take down walls or rip up floors to discover the beauty buried underneath, understanding that a house's true self—its identity and its history—doesn't need to be hidden. With love and an understanding of what it needs, it can become beautiful again.

We are all old houses, altered by time and circumstances. Our lives are shaped by the good and the bad, and we take it all in and make it a part of us.

As it turns out, the things we thought were true, that we thought had branded us for life, weren't so permanent. They were rough drafts, versions of ourselves that were critical to who we are today and are still buried underneath. And the setbacks weren't setbacks at all: they were catalysts. We are always launching ourselves anew.

We've been built up on the cornerstone of family and determination and faith and deep, abiding love, and because of that we are capable and worthy of repurpose, of restoration. Nothing is lost. We can all be made good again.

I sit at the old oak teacher's desk in our office as I have done every day for the past eight years to write the day's entry. This is my ritual, and it has required work. Ben never loses sight of the good in front of us; he believes that everything that has happened is for a worthwhile purpose. His is a natural kind of optimism, whereas mine has required conditioned effort. It's not my natural state, never has been.

Years ago, I made a promise to myself. A pledge to seek out the positive. To take the messiness of life and pull out the thing that made me smile. It took the form of an online journal that I kept every day for eight straight years, which I called "Make Something Good Today."

I vowed to consciously document the best thing that happened every day of my sometimes ho-hum, sometimes magical life. Most days were spent combating my natural disposition to worry and anxiety, but in between burned bright moments that I refused to let slip through the cracks. The journal was designed as an exercise in the power of selective memory.

Writing was a performative act; I wasn't just passively recording what happened but also actively choosing what had happened. What would be imprinted. What was worthy of permanence and what could be discarded. It could be something as simple as the way tree branches looked in the light or a piece of strawberry pie or something larger, such as finishing a house or an elaborate surprise Ben had planned to cheer me up. On bad days, I'd consciously try to search out the positive or make good things happen so I wouldn't be empty-handed at night when it came time to write. In this way, the practice has changed my life.

In the days since it started, people I've loved have died, Ben and I have argued and hurt each other, business has been bad, I've felt uninspired, I've worried about things out of my control. But I have to make the conscious decision to forget those things, to swim in the messiness of life. I have chosen to be kind to people who aren't kind to me, to proactively do, find, and be whatever it is that gives me joy rather than just wish for it.

I make a space where the beautiful moments will live, undisturbed. Later, after time has smoothed over the bumps, it'll seem as though those moments filled all of it, leaving no room for the sad memories. It is an exercise in focusing on what matters in the time I have to spend on this earth, in this body. The hope is that one day this perspective will become so automatic and natural that I will no longer have to write it down.

But when that day comes, I'll have these words and stories and pictures of when Ben and I were young and in love and figuring out how to become who we are, when he and I were just two and not three or four. And I'll be glad that I tracked those gifts along the way, created my own little corner of immortality.

When you document every single day of your life, you're forced to notice the pattern of blessings. In the aftermath of despair, you find the gift of perspective. At a time in my life when nothing was certain, I required a mountain of evidence to truly believe my glass was half full. If I had never started the journal, I would have missed so much.

My life was damaged by childhood bullies, by doubts about my future path, by soul-numbing work that was feeding on me instead of me on it, by a mysterious illness that burdened me for a decade, by bouts of uncertainty that seemed to show up like the seasons. Ben thought he knew his purpose, but there were times when he was piddling in life, unsure what he was meant to do here, what He had meant for him to do.

Life is going to throw curveballs at you. And as you move out of the way, you may get nailed with a fastball. That's what it does. But we have the choice. Because of my childhood I've always been drawn to the unloved and forgotten. Because of Ben's, he's always made the most of what he had, turned it into something valuable, something worth keeping and protecting. Those two things have united in what we currently do in our work. It only makes sense that they would have come together.

When Ben and I look back on our lives, we can see that this has always been the case. We have each made different paths but somehow united in our search to take what is good inside of us, what loves and is loved, and spread it outward. To make something good with what we have, to share in any way we can, and, hopefully, to inspire others to do the same.

Books and stuffed animals. My best friends in childhood.

1

A Girl

Erin

Decide what to be and go be it.
— THE AVETT BROTHERS

Sometimes becoming who we're supposed to be means building walls around ourselves. We grow protective of what we are, afraid the world will not open its arms.

As we age, our differences form our identities, set us apart, become something to be treasured. But when we are young, they are treated as liabilities. They're like scars people point at, laugh at, attack us for having. And they mark us in a way that never quite goes away.

Though nothing ever broke me, a lot of it bruised.

I was an introverted child, sensitive and overly imaginative, and most kids didn't quite know how to take me. Some of them laughed at me, excluded me, bullied me for never quite fitting in. Fitting in was unnatural to me, and I felt punished for failing at it. I didn't know the right jokes to tell, the right things to like, the right way to blend in in our little rural town. It was embarrassing to have no idea how to relate, to feel as though I spoke an entirely different language.

And because I stuck out, and because adolescent girls feel the need to fit in at all costs, I was the easiest to keep out of the inner circle. To feel that you're weird or unlovable by people your own age is to feel like an ugly duck, off in some fundamental way. It crushed me. In a small town, it can be harder; there aren't as many options. Outside of my friend Kandace, whom I'd grown up with in church, I was lonely. When I was very young, I coped by being quiet around kids my age. I dragged my tattered yellow blanket to school because it smelled like waffles and syrup and my mother's perfume.

I would bury my nose in my *Goosebumps* books

or play dodgeball with the boys, who seemed to care less that I was different. But it broke my heart that the girls wanted nothing to do with me: girls who didn't know how cool Mattie in *True Grit* was and didn't collect arrowheads from their grandparents' garden.

I remember a sleepover at a girl's house in fourth grade. I was a little shy about it—I never liked sleeping away from home—but I was excited just to be invited to something. Early in the evening, everyone decided to play hide-and-seek. Before I knew what was happening, the pack of girls called out "You're it!" and one told me to go to her bedroom, shut the door, and count to a hundred. I did as I was told and leaned up against the closed door, counting in anticipation.

When I came out, they were all gone. They had quietly sneaked out—every last one of them—to a neighbor girl's house. It was all a joke on me. It stung worse than not having been invited at all, to be the thing sacrificed to make their fun possible. I felt small and stupid; it confirmed that there must be something wrong with me. I couldn't for the life of me figure out what I'd done wrong, why they didn't want to be my friend.

When I called Mama in tears and asked her to bring me home, she said all the right things. "You are different from those kids," she had told me more than once, "and it will set your life apart in all the best ways." I couldn't see that back then because what nine-year-old can? Children have no choice but to look to other children—who are just as con-

fused and just as scared. That's the problem: kids are the cruelest mirrors.

As the baby of my family, I struggled to relate to people my age, so I became a teacher's pet—connecting with those closer in age to my parents and aunts and uncles. Though my family made me feel less lonely, they couldn't take away the feeling that I didn't belong.

On a sixth-grade field trip to Washington, D.C., many parents, including mine, came along. Mississippi was just so far from the "center of things" that the chance to step into the story of America drew everyone.

I was so excited that morning, having to wake up long before the sun, the day full of possibility. As I nervously boarded the whale of a bus, my eyes went hunting, hoping to find someone to sit with for the eighteen-hour ride. I searched for a friendly face, eyes of recognition, or maybe even a smile. Row by row I asked awkwardly, quietly, if I could sit beside this girl or that one. Again and again I heard "This seat's saved," or witnessed the dropping of pillows on empty seats, the staring out of windows, the ignoring me as though I weren't there. Each rejection was like a sharp cut, embarrassing me in a way that felt like the world would end.

Then, at the back of the bus, I found my parents.

Mama made room for me, reassuring me quietly without saying a word. I sat there soaking in shame as the bus pulled away. I knew better than to shed any tears, so I held them back, heavy as they were.

ABOVE: Fifth grade at Powers Elementary.

I stared out the window and thanked God for my parents, who loved me even if other children did not. Mama reminded me again that I was different—but in the best way possible. And one day, she said, the world would catch up.

Some of the bullying I endured was probably the learned kind, as my parents didn't quite fit in themselves. At my rural school, it was unusual that my dad was a doctor of physical therapy and a department head at our hospital working around the clock so that Mama could be at home with us and do real estate part-time. She drove an imported sedan and played tennis in town, which was also unusual, but there was not the slightest air of snobbery about either of them. Like many of my schoolmates' mothers, Mama had chosen starting a family over finishing college, but still, like me, she stuck out among her rural peers.

Glamorous though she was, she'd also been a tomboy from the day she was born, both tender-hearted and tough. She got her hands dirty helping Daddy keep up our home in the country, tak-

ing care of our chicken farm, putting up corn and peas for the winter, canning fig and pear preserves, sewing, and writing a newspaper column when the time or inspiration presented itself. When a didapper was eating all the bream and catfish in our lake, ruining Daddy's fishing and getting him riled up, she grabbed his shotgun and solved the problem. Mama would not be pinned down.

Mama kept me together. She was my dearest friend, a creative and beautiful soul who encouraged the artist in me from a young age. She had the wisdom and vision to see that I lived in my imagination because that was the only place I felt safe, and she helped expand that part of me. Through her encouragement I learned the power in taking what I had and making something good out of it.

We assembled natural history museums from her riding boot boxes with acrylic paint and my toy dinosaurs. We painted and made papier-mâché masks, clay hand puppets, and tiger and crocodile costumes. Mama helped feed and free a part of me that would otherwise have been locked up, undiscovered and left to rot away. It was encouraged in our house to sing and play music, too. I performed concerts on top of the deep freeze in the darkened laundry room, a flashlight as my spotlight, singing songs from *The Lion King*.

My imagination extended into my circle of friends, so as a child my toys filled in the gaps where other kids might have been. My stuffed animals were the only ones who wouldn't reject me or make me feel lesser for just being me. Bear was my best, most loyal friend. He had a black puppy's nose and spots of matted fur where I'd dropped

ABOVE: Mama and Daddy in the early 90s. I was positive they were Indiana Jones and Princess Diana.

I loved making costumes.

glue or candy on him. He was perfect in his imperfection.

We would lie on the living room floor together eating macaroni and cheese and watching *Fraggle Rock*. He accompanied me onstage in the school play because I was too afraid to go up there alone. At bedtime, in the terrifying darkness and despite what we'd endured that day, Bear would assure me that nothing could hurt us. And I believed him.

I carried an imagination that was big enough to see past the mean, the ugly, and the difficult. I held tight to my mama's vision of me, even against the available evidence, just as I can see today what once was perfect in run-down old buildings.

* * *

My daddy could do everything. He became one of Mississippi's first doctors of physical therapy and started the rehabilitation program at our hospital at the age of twenty-two. When I was very young, he also owned a chicken farm behind our house, a brick ranch-style home built by my grandfather. The chicken trucks would come in the middle of the night, and my mama was so outdone. "I hate it, Phil," she'd say after another night of restless sleep. "It stinks."

"Sure does," he'd say. "Smells like money."

On Saturday trips to town with Daddy I would hide in castles of stacked tires at Sears and sing old country songs in the cab of his old F-150 with him and my older brother, Clark.

Like, really really loved making costumes.

Daddy was stern and conservative, quiet and practical. His deep faith in God made him stronger than all of us put together. His blind devotion to Ole Miss football and overwhelming love for Conway Twitty made him lovably human. If one of his songs came on, Daddy would freely sing, unashamed, no matter who was around. As though he couldn't help it. As though he'd been moved beyond his control.

I had other family surrounding me and supporting me, too, like Mama's sisters, Mae and Phyllis. Aunt Mae would take me to explore the woods in search of fossils and to the library for summer reading and Moon Pies. Then back home to her drafty old Victorian farmhouse to watch John Wayne movies.

She lived on the same land as my mama's parents, Meemaw and Peepaw. I inherited my introversion from Meemaw, and Mae and I would spend quiet afternoons helping her water her many flowers and plants, inviting her along on our nature walks. Meemaw taught me the delicious secret of snapping an aloe pod in half to rub onto and soothe a burned finger.

Peepaw was jovial and incredibly handsome. He was gentlemanly, smelling of Old Spice aftershave, and his shirtsleeves covered the dark blue tattoos of anchors and serpents that wrapped his biceps, along with a heart around my grandmother's name. He could cuss like the sailor he was, but the passage of time and the church had smoothed his rough edges.

Aunt Phyllis lived next door to us and was always spoiling me when she had the chance. In her living room I would build a mountain of blankets

and pillows in the glow of the Disney Channel as I snacked on dill pickles. She'd take me shopping in town with my cousin Kelsa, and if she saw me looking at a toy or book, she'd buy it on the sly and surprise me with it in the car.

Mammaw and Pappaw, my father's parents, lived just through the woods from our house and often watched me. Sometimes I'd cry when my parents dropped me off, but within minutes Mammaw would make me forget. She'd pull the red-and-white-striped blanket, thin as a tablecloth, out of the linen closet, and we'd build a fort in the dining room. I was an odd child in that I didn't like sweets, so afterward we would make cookies out of pie crust that tasted like Ritz crackers.

ABOVE: Peepaw looked like George Clooney! That's Meemaw Jack under his arm, though her first name was actually Helen.

When it got colder, she would take my cousin Jim and me into the backyard and make a ring of bricks in which to build a campfire. We would roast hot dogs while she and Pappaw told us scary stories. After my bubble bath, they would watch *Hee Haw* while I read the *Reader's Digest* version of *The Swiss Family Robinson*. When I got sleepy, I'd crawl into the pink cotton sheets of the guest bed, musty like baby powder and dust. Mammaw knew I was afraid of the dark in their house, so she would sleep beside me with the covers pulled all the way over her face—it's how she liked to sleep.

Home was with my family, was where I played and laughed and loved and was accepted. It planted a seedling in me about what family can do and what it's supposed to be. And as I got older, I would always be looking for that same feeling out in the world.

As I grew up, I stood more comfortably in my shoes, caring less about the insiders who saw me as little more than an outsider. I also began to realize what everyone knows about bullies: they're desperate to be liked and dying to belong. They use meanness as a way to feel included. As I came into my own, standing sturdier on my own two feet, I found space in my heart to feel sorry for them.

While most of my classmates were sneaking Miller Lites to the pasture parties after the football game, I picked up a guitar and started singing at the coffee shop in downtown Laurel where I worked. I found a world of confidence as a musician, and performing became my life. When I first went onstage, I embraced the idea of becoming someone else. But pretty quickly I grew into being myself. It was as though I were shedding skin up there. Once again, I held tight and fast to things about myself that I liked, found the things about the world I wanted to swim in, and dived in headfirst.

There were only eight miles between where I lived in Jones County and the town of Laurel, but they were worlds apart. To a county kid, Laurel proper was an exotic place, and I was jealous of my friends who got to live there. The homes were old, classic, and mysterious, nothing like the midcentury ranch houses in the county. There was the art museum we'd visit on field trips, historic

ABOVE: Pappaw and Mammaw and some of their close, warm personal friends.

My First Reveal Day

I remember the weekend in seventh grade when Mama and I redecorated my bedroom exactly as I pleased, choosing a cloud wallpaper for the ceiling in my desk nook.

We framed my artwork from school: huge, primitive, gestural black sketches of birds and fish that I watercolored in abstract washes, inspired by Walter Anderson. Art brought out a hidden me and helped me find my voice. With my mother, in those quiet rooms, I could even create a new self. That weekend with Mama, given all the creative license I could ever ask for, was the beginning of my love for home design.

streetlights instead of industrial "booger" lights high on wooden posts, sidewalks and avenues instead of roads and ditches.

We were Baptists, and though I loved the people of our church, I struggled with some of the more strict stances on the music and art that made me feel like I had found myself. I held fast to the things that weren't embraced there, believing they were a way out. When I was young, I had carried fear and shame for not being able to measure up to others, never really wanting to or knowing how. As I grew up, my freedom came from letting them go. I had dreams of breaking out, leaving the small-town life behind, and making it in a city as an artist, a place that would inspire and embrace me in a way that Jones County, Mississippi, simply could not.

I had grown up visiting St. Augustine, Florida, the oldest city in the United States, a place where both my daddy and my brother had gone to school. They'd learned their professions in the Old City, and for a time, I'd thought that was my destiny as well. On family trips I fell in love with Flagler College, which stands regally in the center of town. As a young girl I made a plan to go there, to make it my launching pad into a bigger and brighter life.

Flagler College was a former hotel with spires and courtyards, L. C. Tiffany glass windows surrounding a dining hall that reminded me of what you'd find on Ivy League campuses. I knew in my gut that if I could be surrounded by that kind of earnest history, by the craftsmanship and the beauty, I would be a better artist.

Flagler was hugged on all four sides by stucco buildings from the 1700s with clay tile roofs and coquina shell walls that had withstood cannonballs and two centuries of hurricanes and wars. The location was romantic, but on a practical level, it meant that space for students was limited. Even with a 3.9 GPA, my going there was not to be, and the rejection was something I carried heavily for some time. But it didn't break me; my imagination was too large for my hometown, and I would find a way to make use of it.

As a teenager, I saw Tim Burton's *Big Fish*, a film about a dying father, Edward Bloom, whose tall tales inspired his wayward son, and it

FLAGLER COLLEGE
OFFICE OF ADMISSIONS

March 10, 2003

Laurel, MS

Dear Erin:

I am writing to inform you that we no longer have space available to accommodate you for the term which begins in September 2003. I regret to advise you that we cannot offer you admission other than on a waiting list status.

I know that this may come as a disappointment to you, because you are a good student and because you meet our standards for admission. I also realize that it may be difficult to understand why we are unable to offer you a space in the class, when you meet our qualifications for admission.

By way of explanation, you need to know that Flagler College is small by intent with the enrollment limited by the Board of Trustees to approximately 1900 students. In order to stay within this planned enrollment, we must place certain limits on the size of the incoming class. Unfortunately, because of our self-imposed limit on enrollment and because of the size of our applicant pool, we cannot offer admission to all applicants who are qualified for admission.

To date, we have received more than five applications for every space available in the incoming class. Based on previous years' experience, we know that we can offer admission to less than one-third of the candidates who apply for admission if we hope to keep our enrollment at or below the desired level.

We regret we cannot offer you a space in the class at this time; however, because you meet our standards for admission, you have been placed on a waiting list for the term beginning September 2003. The waiting list status means that you meet the standards for admission but we are unable to accommodate you because of the large number of qualified candidates applying for admission.

P.O. BOX 1027 • ST. AUGUSTINE • FLORIDA 32085-1027 • 800-304-4208 • 904-829-6481 • www.flagler.edu

The best thing that ever happened to me was a rejection letter.

I wanted hair like Ani DiFranco's, but I was too straight-edge to go all the way. So I compromised by wearing braids for a few weeks. Oh, to be a teenager.

For my senior trip, my parents gave me a suitcase with vintage postcards printed all over it and told me I could choose anywhere on the bag. I chose San Francisco. Mama snapped this photo of me there, in Amoeba Music.

became my favorite movie of all time. As I watched it in the theater, I immediately recognized Bloom as Hollywood's version of Pappaw, who had passed away from ALS when I was fifteen. To this day, people still recount stories to me that my grandfather told them—and he comes alive for me again.

The thing I loved most about the movie was Edward's capacity to see the magic in the mundane, to mythologize it, to turn the ordinary into the extraordinary. His ambition, coupled with imagination, meant that no matter where life took him, the magic was inside of him. Whatever happened was worth turning into a fable and putting back out into the world.

My imagination as a child ran deep and wild, and it's still there, making my life better or worse, depending on the day. It serves me well when I see the beautiful future of a long-unloved house; other times it makes me feel terrified, and certain, that everything's going to crash on top of me.

I grew a thicker skin, but I still didn't have faith that life wouldn't always be so lonely. I wondered what else was out there—hoping, dreaming that there were more people who would embrace me for my differences, a career that would inspire me, and a purpose that would be as strong and illuminating as the bright sun.

I resolved to make my own way, to put myself out into the world, trusting and praying that the dreams I had for my life would all come true. That I would indeed make something good out of this life. All in due time.

Clark, Mama, and Daddy with me at
High school graduation, 2003

I don't think Daddy realized we were taking a picture, and this makes me laugh.

The Dodge was Daddy's winch truck. During Desert Storm, he hauled scrap iron to make ends meet.
This was the Fourth of July parade when we lived in Sumrall, Mississippi.

2

A Boy

Ben

I grew up with three brothers, who doubled as my best friends, so I never had to worry about having someone to sit next to.

In fact, I probably took it for granted that there would always be a seat for me. I had friends growing up, but it's different when you have brothers. Everybody else is just kind of passing through.

Since we moved around a lot, I never got too attached to friends; there was never enough time for friendships to stick and settle, the way they need to. It's not that we were insular. It was just that we were the Napiers and we felt we had all we needed.

My family gave me a feeling of invincibility that I then brought forward into the world. I've always been quick to start a conversation and unafraid to put myself out there. Nothing could touch me, because I was one of the Napier Boys. That didn't mean we could get away with anything, because we most certainly could not. My parents always held us to an extremely high standard; so much of what is good in my life I owe to them, the way they made sure I could clear that height.

I got my name from my mom's father, Benjamin Luke Pickering, and my work ethic and confidence from a line of hardworking Scottish farmers who crossed the Atlantic centuries ago. It was nurtured by my parents, high school sweethearts from south Mississippi who thought the sun rose and set in each other's eyes. My mother is a quirky, brilliant, and empathetic woman who raised us four boys to know right from wrong. My father is a strong, romantic bull of a man with a whip-smart mind and huge, rough hands like catcher's mitts.

Because we lived in so many different places, the only constant was one another. Our six-person unit was home, and we could pick up and move it anywhere. It gave me a feeling of safety and security because wherever we moved, I had a built-in circle and a protective shield.

We were all fairly sheltered growing up, by circumstance more than by design. All we knew was what was going on in our house. That was all we needed.

Sam was four years older and the ultimate older brother, with an outgoing manner and a natural intelligence. He was tall and rail thin, an exceptional athlete, and he bullied and protected his younger brothers in equal measure.

Tom was two years younger than me, relatively a late bloomer in size and essentially my double. We were "the boys," as in "Where are Sam and the boys?" and if one was doing something, the other was always there—for better or worse. We played basketball and rode four-wheelers, built trucking empires with our Tonkas, and acted out Wild West cowboy stories in our various backyards across Mississippi.

My baby brother, Jesse, was ten years younger and had the luxury of being raised by all of us. He had the creativity and imagination of an only child because of the wide age gap between us. I have memories of listening for him in the bath and hearing him having entire conversations with himself in there, building stories out of thin air. I'm sure he got the worst of the bullying, and after years of putting up with it, he became bulletproof to anyone's ribbing.

From our dad we learned to be compassionate, to flirt, to tell big stories, and to drive fast. Most behavior fell under a simple test: if we didn't see Daddy doing it, then we didn't need to do it. Though we're all built for football, Daddy didn't play—his school had been too small to have a team—so neither did we. Instead it was basketball we loved, and we were

TOP LEFT: Working on eighteen-wheelers was fun, not work, to my brothers and me.
TOP RIGHT: Mama holding me, with Sam beside us.
BOTTOM LEFT: Tom, Jesse in Sam's lap, and me. | BOTTOM RIGHT: When I think of Daddy in my childhood, this is what I see.

always watching *Hoosiers* or reenacting one of its scenes. I never tasted alcohol because Daddy didn't drink. I was never instructed not to; we just followed his example. No smoking, no tattoos, no drugs—none of that. My dad told me he didn't do those things because "your mom and you boys are about all I can afford." To this day, I haven't ever tasted alcohol. Never tried it. Never needed it.

Daddy was tall and heavyset, with broad shoulders, massive arms, and a barrel chest. To us, he was like the living embodiment of every hero in every movie we ever watched: the cowboy, the fast driver, the sheriff, the genius.

When we were very young, my dad lost our farm, a hard bottom that must've been cruel and difficult for him, married with three young children. But he only came back stronger. For fifteen years, he clawed his way back, doing every odd job he could to make ends meet, all kinds of backbreaking manual labor: roughnecking in the oil field, logging, farming, and driving a truck.

Daddy had a kind and gentle soul but would whip an ass if he needed to, especially to protect or stand up for those he cared about. His fearlessness was legendary, and we'd gather around in awe to hear stories about him: how he'd once accidentally pulled the steel handle off a truck like Superman, how he'd chased down a thief stealing his truck decals and sat on him until help came. People would see Daddy fix something or figure something out, and they'd let us know how smart he was, how lucky we were that he would impart some of his knowledge to us.

My mother was beautiful, six feet tall with long, dark hair in big curls. She was the perfect partner for my dad, and he treated her like a queen. Their love for each other was so present and obvious, it was like a light running through our home.

She was the kind of mother who treated us like adults in the making, engaging us in deep topics before we might have a chance to stray off course. In first grade I'd bring up girls, and she'd look at me and get serious pretty quickly.

"Now, Ben, girls are okay," she'd say. "You don't need to be grossed out by them."

"Yes, ma'am."

"Always be nice to them, and one day you'll find the girl you'll always want to talk to. That's how you'll know that's the one you want to spend the rest of your life with."

"Yes, ma'am."

"You have a lot of love to give, Ben," Mama said in her smooth voice. "And whoever that girl is, she'll be lucky to find it."

It was big-picture stuff, maybe even heavy to a seven-year-old, but coming from her, it didn't seem so. It felt as though she was teaching us the laws of nature, and we listened. It was like that about everything—being careful with money and paying attention and working hard in school.

ABOVE: My parents met in high school. Daddy was about to walk onto the basketball court when he saw Mama sitting in the bleachers with some guy she was there on a date with. As the game was about to start, he strode up the bleachers taking them two at a time, took off his class ring and his watch, handed them to Mama, and said, "Hang on to this for me." The Napier men are not lacking in confidence.

Exotica Food Corporation

When we were growing up, my parents would let us boys get creative in the kitchen under their guidance. The gourmet dishes we created became part of what is known to my family as the "Exotica Food Corporation." Here's a sampling of the cuisine:

*Fried Chicken Rolls
Ingredients:
White bread
Butter
Cinnamon
Sugar
Spread butter on bread, sprinkle on cinnamon and sugar, toast. Enjoy.

*Why is it called Fried Chicken Rolls? Easy. My older brother, Sam, thought fried chicken was good and rolls were good . . . And so was this.

Cow Stuff
Ingredients:
Pot roast beef
Gravy (homemade)
Mashed potatoes (real ones)
*Cheese
Mix ingredients together. Serve. Enjoy.

*Cheese does not always come with Cow Stuff, but you can add it if you want. That's what makes it the Exotica Food Corporation Freedom.

Mama really domesticated us, despite Daddy's inclination and efforts to let us run wild. Growing up, we learned how to cook, iron our shirts, do laundry, wash dishes, clean a home properly. Besides not doing what Daddy didn't do, the other big rule was: we were always to mind Mama. There was nothing that would get us into trouble quicker than crossing her. If Daddy found out that we hadn't set the table or loaded the dishwasher after Mama had told us to, there was a problem. In our household, they were a united front.

> There was no going to ask Mama if you could do something if Daddy said you couldn't and vice versa. They were like two halves of the same whole.

Mama had her hands full feeding all of us: making scrambled eggs and bacon or oatmeal in the morning, a big supper every single night of the week. It was weird to see on TV or read about families no longer eating around the dinner table or eating in front of the TV. We always sat around the table, said a prayer, and then ate as a family. There was no designated night for it—it was every night of the week.

And every meal was a feast. Mama is an incredible cook, a master at figuring out what she can make from what she has in the pantry. I learned from her to make do with what you have. Most incredibly, she would do it all without a recipe. The knowledge was just in her.

What stands out in my memory is Mama's mastery of gravy: brown, white, pepper, tomato. She'd put it on mashed potatoes with hamburger steak or on rice next to a roast. To this day, I'll eat just about anything with her gravy on it.

Like every other southern woman, she also makes biscuits, which are peculiar in that they're square. In the mornings she had to make eggs and bacon for five of us, so she'd just roll the dough to fit into a square pan and then cut them out. For birthdays she always made delicious cakes from scratch, which I didn't even appreciate until I was older. By then I'd had enough store-bought cakes that I knew the difference. None of them was like Mama's.

Every day when we came home from school, Mama was there. She went to all our basketball games, school functions, and parent-teacher meetings. She never missed a thing, and I felt secure that she never would.

As far as we were concerned, though we had little, our parents were royalty and the only currency that mattered in our home was their approval. The best way to earn it, we knew, was if someone outside of the family bragged on us—how we were respectful or hardworking. That would make our parents the proudest.

It was never spoken, but we always had to behave in public because we were representing our family. We were to be respectful of everyone, whether rich or poor, male or female, black or white. It did not matter. We always shook hands, kept eye contact, stood up straight, never with our hands in our pockets, said, "Yes, sir," "No, sir," "Yes, ma'am," and "No, ma'am." Some of it was taught to us, but most of it we learned just from watching Mama and Daddy.

Even when my parents punished us, no matter how bad we were or how bad the punishment was, Daddy would make us look him in the eye and would tell us, "I'm doing this because I love you and I want you to be a better man." That was ingrained in us. I remember rolling my eyes at my math teacher once and getting slapped by my mother. The pain of upsetting her hurt more than the sting of her hand.

It couldn't have been easy for my parents, but they never let the strain show, at least not to us boys. As I grew up, I learned to feel for them in ways a kid couldn't, recognizing things that I'd never noticed. I couldn't imagine what feeding six of us must've cost, but they'd somehow pulled it off. I guess that's part of what parents do: they shield you from the heavy realities they're carrying on their backs. Like ducks swimming in a pond—calm and collected above the water but underneath, treading like hell.

Daddy first felt the call to be a minister when he was in high school riding on my grandfather's tractor. He did not heed the call then, and by the time I was born, he had actually moved away from the church entirely. He wasn't mad at God or anything, he just fell away through circumstance and his busy work life.

There was no mountaintop moment for me in regard to the church. It was just the air I breathed from the beginning. My whole life, we had a relationship with God and Christ. I never doubted it, questioned it, or had any reason to.

As far back as I can remember, my mom would take me and my brothers to church on Sundays. For many years my dad would stay home, working on his eighteen-wheelers in the driveway. That's how it is if you own your vehicle in the trucking industry: it's your livelihood, so you drive six days a week and spend the seventh making sure it'll stay running.

The preacher at our church, D. R. "Raggy" Ragsdale, was a joyful person with thinning gray hair and blue eyes. When he wasn't in the pulpit, he would dress in old linen and twill shirts, broken-in blue jeans, and tennis shoes. He never wore the robe and stole unless it was for a wedding or a funeral, though I never saw him on Sunday morning without a suit and tie. He was an amazing guitar player and a playful guy who reminded me of Robin Williams, the way he used crazy voices and characters to entertain young and old parishioners alike.

Every Saturday, Raggy, who lived next door, would come out and talk with Daddy. Raggy never brought up faith or the church, choosing instead just to bombard him with questions about what he was up to and anything about cars because he didn't know a thing. There was no agenda behind it; Raggy was just a friendly guy, we were next-door neighbors in a small town, and Daddy would talk to anyone.

One Sunday morning when I was six, Tom asked my dad to come to church with us. Something about his four-year-old's request broke my dad's heart; he got dressed, joined us for church, and hasn't missed a Sunday since. Once he started going, he was all in: he became extremely involved in the church, the services, Bible study, fund-raisers, singing in the choir, driving the church bus, everything.

When I was in sixth grade, I guess the call got loud enough. Daddy sold his truck and our farm, went back to college, and became a minister. I was in awe of that. He was doing well, had four kids at home and a wife and a farm and a good job, and he gave it all up to follow that calling. He got a job as a minister, so we all moved to Buckatunna, Mississippi, which is just a wide spot in the road on Highway 45, the most rural place we'd ever lived in. But I had a deep love of small towns and the country life. Wherever we went, Mama and Daddy would try to bring the community together and we would try to make the place our own.

I was now a preacher's kid, so as I grew up I took on more responsibilities. As a teenager I was always at the church doing some menial task, such as turning on the lights or heat for the women's circle, singing in the Christmas cantatas at the church, spending my summers at church camp and my breaks at vacation Bible school with the younger kids even when I got older, and even filling in for the

ABOVE: I am very good at tying a tie. There are about a million church portraits of my brothers and me just like this one, every year of our life. I'm on the left, Jesse is at the bottom, Tom is on the right, Sam is standing behind us.

Granddaddy, Jesse, Daddy, and me at Daddy's graduation from Duke. My grandparents made the trip up from Mississippi, and Jesse will be really pleased I included this photo of him in his Bobby Hill stage. I was loading trucks on the night shift at UPS then, the one-year gap between high school and college.

youth minister my senior year in high school. I was connected to my faith, and I took it seriously, but I never saw it as a calling. It was just what I did.

As I was starting high school, Daddy finished his undergraduate degree and we picked up and moved to North Carolina so he could get his master's at Duke—the school whose basketball team we'd idolized our whole lives. In less than a decade, Daddy had gone from being elbow deep in the black grease of diesel engines, hauling scrap iron for extra money, to attending one of the finest schools in the nation. But he still spent his Saturdays working on engines so we could get to church every Sunday.

By the age of sixteen, I was going out more with friends, though my parents kept me rooted the best they could. I would miss only one family dinner a week and avoided doing anything my dad wouldn't do.

When I graduated from high school, I was set on going to junior college back in Mississippi, where I'd accumulated a few friends over our years there. Daddy convinced me to hold off a year until he had graduated and they all moved back south. I took a job loading trucks on the night shift at UPS that year and saved up money. When we did go back, the family moved to north Mississippi, almost five hours away from my college, as far away as they could be while still being in the state.

I wouldn't say I rebelled at Jones County Junior College, though the freedom and distance from my parents did allow me to slack off

The Chevelle

Throughout my entire childhood, my dad helped a friend keep his 1969 Chevelle running, until eventually Daddy bought it from him. My brothers and I all helped him turn wrenches on it whenever we could. When we were growing up, that old car was the only constant in our lives besides our parents. Even

when we moved across the country, we dragged the old Chevelle with us. After all these years, we've still not finished fixing it up because of the constant upheaval that comes with being the family of an itinerant pastor. But one day, it'll shine again.

TOP LEFT: Me on the left, Jesse on the right, Tom standing—Easter 2001, a few years after Sam had gone off to school.
TOP RIGHT: Casual senior portrait, 2002, casually relaxing on nondescript acid-washed blobs.
BOTTOM: Senior prom with my friend, who was the Belgian foreign-exchange student.

more on my studies than I'm proud to admit. I kept my grades from them and never felt good about it. They had taught me to be open and honest and to value my education, and I guess I was worried I was letting them down.

Being away from home was tough, especially at first. My family, particularly my brother Tom, was such a huge part of my identity that it felt as though part of me was split off. Plus I couldn't afford a cell phone back then, so I went from talking to my parents and brothers every day to checking in maybe once a month. I honestly felt some guilt over it, but I also saw how it was good for me. I was breaking free from my shelter, which had sustained me but had also prevented me from discovering who I was on my own.

At college, I got to work building a community like the one my family had always been, like the kind Daddy had helped to build in the small towns where he preached. I would find people, make a life away from my brothers that felt much the same. I would be everybody's friend. And while it was never my intent to settle down in college, with so many girls to meet and the freedom to do as I pleased, I wasn't long from meeting a girl like the one Mama had described. The girl I would never want to stop talking to.

ABOVE: Jesse, Sam, Tom, me, and wood paneling.

Spring 2006, from a photo booth at a pub in Oxford. Junior year of college.

3

A Love Story

Ben

At Jones County Junior College, I was having more fun sober than most people were having drunk.

Having grown up relatively sheltered, I had a mind to soak it all up and get to know as many people as I could. College was a constant, twenty-four-hour, all-you can-eat buffet, and I ate it up.

Though I kissed my share of girls, I never got serious with any of them. I would have had a 4.0 GPA if flirting was a major, and would help the girls I'd once dated jump off their car or join them for a study group after the interest wore thin. But I never met a girl I liked more than I liked being untethered.

I did what I could to suck the marrow out of life and was up for anything, anytime. My friends knew that about me. In fact, just about everybody on campus did. My buddies and I would spend a night on

Bourbon Street in New Orleans singing karaoke with a bachelorette party, cross the Pontchartrain at sunrise, and make it back to campus five minutes before my 8 a.m. class.

I had absolutely no money and drove a rusty 1983 Chevy Suburban my buddies and I called Dale. He was the size and color of a battleship, with a Jolly Roger flying from the back bumper. I mixed a few nicer items in with my thrift store clothes. I lived in an old, gray, run-down, condemnable house on campus with my two best friends. There were nickel-sized gaps around the windows and rust in the cast-iron bathtub, but man, we felt like kings.

ABOVE: December 7, 2004. The day I first spent time with Erin. I was at a party later that night.

TOP: The Grey House, my home in college. The subfloors were rotting in the laundry room, and we didn't go on the porch because it might collapse.
BOTTOM LEFT: At an Ole Miss football game.
BOTTOM RIGHT: Leading the student section at a football game.

Erin

Independence is more a state of mind than anything else. Jones County Junior College was only twenty minutes away from home, but it felt it could be hours. Though I missed my parents—and visited them twice a week—the freedom of living on my own brought me a new kind of happiness. My bad attitude about going to Jones over Flagler vanished because I realized that college was college and I would make the most of it. That's what I was good at— using my imagination to see the beauty in the ordinary, to bloom where I was planted.

I was excited to get busy making my own way in the world, bent on making the absolute most of the art courses and of designing the college yearbook, which I approached as though it were a national magazine. I still had big dreams of being a graphic designer for a publisher or ad agency, hopefully in a big city, maybe far away from the Mississippi I felt I'd outgrown.

At Jones I straddled two worlds. One was filled with student leader types, devout, whole-some kids planning missionary trips to places such as the Philippines or South America. They journaled every morning before class, appreciated art and literature, and were kind and gracious givers. I mostly fit in with them, having never tried any substance stronger than Sudafed. (I still haven't.) One member of that crowd was my best friend from high school, Hope, whom I was still close with, and we traveled the world together performing in the Jones concert choir.

But I considered myself a free spirit, had cut my long hair into a pixie, and also hung out with the creative alternatives who smoked cigarettes and dyed their hair primary colors. I shared their love of indie music, rare in a part of the world saturated in overproduced country music. My friends went to or played shows in New Orleans late on school nights. Sometimes I'd join them, but I was juggling two jobs and devoted to school. Even if I was out until 4 a.m. at a concert, I'd be in class at 8 a.m., ready to take notes.

TOP: My dorm room. I was lucky to be in the brand-new dorms on campus. Quite the opposite of Ben's living arrangements.
BOTTOM: The summer before sophomore year, my friend Micah took this (cheesy) photo and used it to paint a (very cool) portrait.

Ben

At Jones, I tried to create a community by sheer force of will, enthusiasm, and charm. It was a junior college where most of the students went home to their parents' house at the end of the day and on the weekends. But I loved the school so much that I made it my mission to change that. I wanted to have the best time in the world, and I wanted everyone around me to as well.

I'd get people to stay on campus and support the teams by starting student sections at the basketball and football games. I got into student government and joined all the committees on campus: the Fall Freeze Committee, the Spirit Committee, the Bobcat Brigade, anything I could get into, anything that was building or solidifying the college community. It was my first time on my own; my family had been a built-in community for me, and suddenly they weren't there. So I turned Jones into my family. It would be a common theme throughout my life: selecting and bringing people or objects together in a way that made sense, that made people feel good.

Erin

Ben Napier and I circled each other before we ever really met. Actually, it's more accurate to say I circled him, like a moon in his orbit. I admired him from afar, thinking I'd never be the kind of girl he'd notice. I was quiet and didn't seek out the spotlight; that seemed to belong to him. He was tall and broad, bearded, and shaggy-haired in those days, and magnetic, without ever letting it get to his head. Or so I imagined. I didn't actually know him.

I saw him lead the rowdy Fall Freeze midnight breakfast parties, raise money for student government, usually with a beauty queen or cheerleader waiting nearby. I watched him find the one person eating alone in the student union and pull up a chair beside him or her. He was kind to anyone who would allow it and open in a way that few people were. Ben was popular, but not exclusive, and I think that's why I loved him before I even knew him. Even from far away I could feel his joy and generosity.

Ben and I first spoke at a McDonald's just off campus, on the last day of freshman year, May 2004. I was getting my drink from the fountain, nervously aware that he was walking toward me. He had this huge presence that was due only partly to his size. He just occupied space in a way that was unmistakable. It was something I would grow to love, but at that moment I was a little intimidated by it.

"Hey, you're Kristen's roommate!" he said. "I'm Ben." I was frozen by the way he just launched into it like that, like picking up a conversation we had been having.

"Yeah," I said. "I've seen you at school. You sort of look like a guy I work with." I was talking about Charlie, whom I would later briefly date, not coincidentally, because he reminded me a little of Ben Napier.

We seemed to occupy two distant shores of a gigantic sea, much too far to ever cross.

He laughed easily. "Well, then, he must be a pretty good-lookin' guy."

Yes, he is. You smell so good. I think you are wonderful.

"I guess," I sputtered, then smiled barely enough to salvage my lackluster response. I didn't know how else to hide such enormous feelings for a boy who was little more to me than a stranger.

He paused, almost imperceptibly. I couldn't tell if he was insulted or just thinking of something else to say. "All right, well," he sheepishly offered. "Good meeting you," he said in a way that reminded me of Chris Farley's sweet-natured Tommy Callahan. The warmth in his smile remained, as though nothing fazed him, and then he was off.

He wandered back to the pool of his crowd, where he immediately changed the temperature and flow of the water. He was the center of attention no matter where he went, and I kept a cool distance the few times we spoke. I put a lot of energy into pretending I was putting in none. It didn't seem as though it would matter anyway. We seemed to occupy two distant shores of a gigantic sea, much too far to ever cross.

Ben

DECEMBER 6, 2004

In December of sophomore year, a girl I knew from the yearbook asked me if I wanted to participate in an interview series about the most interesting people on campus. I was flattered but felt undeserving. I agreed when I remembered that there was this cute girl on staff I wanted to get to know. Her hair was short and blond like Meg Ryan's, and she wore loose jeans and tight T-shirts that had caught my wandering attention.

I sometimes saw her coming and going from the visual arts building and was especially taken by her walk. She didn't swing her hips the showy way other girls did. Altogether, there was just something about her; I could tell she was different, and I was drawn to that. The one time I flirted with her, she didn't giggle and let me carry on. She kind of shut me down in a heartbeat. Which made me like her even more.

I built up my courage to try again. And this time, she would have to talk to me; I was the feature in a yearbook project. Opportunity knocks but once, so I threw the door wide open.

ABOVE: Erin in England on the JCJC choir tour, spring 2004.

Erin

The idea of spending an afternoon with Ben Napier, whether he paid me any attention or not, would be the highlight of my month. Ben had a joy for life that seemed to spread outward from him. When I walked into the yearbook offices, two girls were laughing and flirting with him. He was wearing a blue T-shirt over white long sleeves, worn-out khaki shorts, and red, white, and blue Adidas sneakers. As I walked by, he reached out for my arm—and I breezily gave him a side hug.

"Two arms, please," he said, and then wrapped me up, my heart racing. For the first time I noticed how very big he was—six feet, six inches tall and nearly 300 pounds. I felt small as a bird. I could smell the laundry detergent he used and his cologne, and I melted.

Once we got talking about the project, it became pretty obvious that he wasn't interested in taking it seriously: it was just another act in the Traveling Ben Napier Show. He told me he wanted to make fun of cheesy portraits where the class president poses beside a lake with a jacket thrown over his shoulder. He shared his idea of dressing like Will Ferrell as Robert Goulet on *Saturday Night Live*, an ugly sweater with a blazer, sunglasses, a pipe, and plenty of pomade. "Why don't we do some shots of me in the lake or something?" he suggested.

"In the lake?" I asked, thinking I misunderstood him.

"Yeah, like actually in it. Standing in it," he said.

After we finished, he asked me to join him for dinner at the student union. I accepted, but once I was sitting across from him, I had to hide that I was too nervous to eat a bite. A few minutes after we sat down, his friends all gathered around, and then a girl sat down and started a conversation with Ben, treating me like the furniture. He talked to her for a minute before she stopped and gave him a look, tilting her head. "Do you know my name, Ben?" she asked.

When he hesitated, and she turned away to speak to a friend walking past, I whispered it under my breath, rescuing him. When the girl left, he smiled at me.

"Thanks for that," he said.

"Sure," I said. "But do you know my name?"

"Of course. Erin Jacqueline Rasberry," he said, with no hesitation. Coming out of his mouth, my name sounded like music. I had to stop myself from asking him to say it again. Charlie, whom I'd been on only a few dates with, hadn't made me feel like that. No boy ever had.

The next morning, my roommate Kristen told me Ben had been texting her all night, which crushed me. I felt somewhat foolish, figuring I was not special after all, that he must give every girl the same attention. I felt a little stupid for falling for it.

Ben

If anyone knew what the situation was between Erin and this Charlie guy, it would be Kristen. I spent the night before texting her, trying to get to the bottom of it, probably giving myself away. But I didn't care—life as I'd known it seemed to fade to gray after Erin showed up blazing in Technicolor.

I arrived at the yearbook offices for the photo shoot in my Goulet outfit, my hair slicked over in a

Goulet Day

The "Goulet Day" picture, two days after the yearbook meeting, four days before "I love you."
Photo by Matt Bush

Drive Safely

My roommate at Jones made this mix CD in 2004 that we passed back and forth, though I eventually became the keeper of it. It stayed in my little blue Volkswagen, and besides Damien Rice's O *album (which there was also a lot of on this CD), this is the only music Ben and I listened to when we first met—over and over and over and over:*

1. Firedoor - Ani DFranco
2. Toxic - Britney Spears
3. Breakaway - Kelly Clarkson
4. Mr. Brightside - The Killers
★ 5. Delicate - Damien Rice
      (our song ♥)
6. The Blower's Daughter - Damien Rice
7. Cannonball - Damien Rice
8. I Remember - Damien Rice
9. Get Gone - Fiona Apple
10. Somewhere Only We Know - Keane
11. This Is the Last Time - Keane
12. Stay - Lisa Loeb
13. Bury Me With It - Modest Mouse
14. The Long Day is Over - Norah Jones
15. You Will be My ain true love - Alison Krauss
16. Mr. Zebra - Tori Amos
17. Hey Jude - The Beatles

hard part. Since I had to go waist deep into the lake, I wore gym shorts and brought along my roommate's girlfriend's Labrador puppy to give the photos an air of sporting sophistication.

"What happened to your legs?" Erin said, looking at the scrapes up and down both of my kneecaps.

Looking at my knees, I said, "Well, I was dressed up like Santa Claus at a Christmas party last night. I might have slid across the floor singing karaoke."

Erin laughed. "You still good with going into the lake?" she asked.

"Yeah," I said, shrugging it off. "A little pond water staph infection won't hurt."

As Erin interviewed me, I could barely pay attention to her questions. I was paying too much attention to her.

At one point, she was looking down at her notes and reading the next question, asking me about my favorite books.

When she looked up, I leaned in and Erin didn't pull away.

"You were going to kiss me," I said.

"What?! No, I wasn't." She claimed to be oblivious.

I didn't kiss her then, but that was the first time I knew I would, sooner or later. It was like gravity, and there was no chance I could stop it.

We all headed out to the lake, where I waded into the freezing water, my knees sinking into the mud. The puppy wriggled, I grinned, they got the photos, and the whole staff headed back to the office for Erin to edit them.

As the day wore on, the crowd dwindled until it was just the two of us. The sun was long gone, and I sat in the plastic chair beside her desk, dripping wet, watching her work. I stayed there, pretending I wanted to see how the photos turned out, but really I just wanted to be near her. I wanted to see how *this* turned out.

After I changed into dry clothes, we got to talking and it came up that my dad had always had us working on cars when we were growing up. She asked me to take a listen to the scraping sound her brakes had been making, and I didn't need her to ask twice.

We took her blue Volkswagen Beetle down the back roads, through the woods, and past the fields that were dead from frost. But her brakes never made a sound. The only sound I remember was the backdrop of the violins from a Damien Rice song on her stereo. We took a ride out to the Sonic for some food and then sat in the car and talked while I watched her nibble mozzarella sticks.

Then my phone started going off with texts from my friends who were headed down to New Orleans.

"So you've got fun plans tonight," she said.

"Not if I can help it," I said, typing a reply.

I told them I wasn't feeling it that night. They must've been shocked.

I never took a pass on those invites; in fact, I was usually the one pushing for the all-nighter, for the girls and the adventure. But I honestly didn't want to go. I wanted to sit in this little blue Bug and talk with this girl. The girl.

We sat in her car and talked for hours. I told her about my three brothers who were like a built-in protective shield, how my dad had become a minister late in life, that I'd kissed more girls than I could count, that I'd never loved any of them, that I hated the new duet with Nelly and Tim McGraw playing on every radio from here to Knoxville. She told me about how creative her mama was, how she hadn't really known her older brother, Clark, until he'd left the house, how her dad was die-hard Ole Miss, how she had kissed exactly five boys, how she hated that song, too.

When we realized the time, she raced back to her dorm for the 12:15 curfew. Nine minutes later we were on the phone, not ready to say good night.

We talked until the sun came up, not a single awkward silence passing between us.

Erin

DECEMBER 9, 2004

"So tell me about this guy you're seeing," Ben said.

It was the next night, and we were seated on the same side of a booth at Sports Rock, a dark and loud club that I'd ordinarily have avoided like the plague. But Ben was the designated driver and had invited me to ride with him so we could keep each other company. Sober buddies.

Earlier that evening, I had been running from dorm room to dorm room looking in my friends' closets for something to wear, trying to find something that said "me"—but the best version of me. The "me" I thought Ben Napier would fall for. I feel as though there's a life lesson buried there because all the searching just led me back to my own closet. I pulled out a slinky black scoop-neck top, dark jeans, and black ballet flats and was checking myself in the mirror when my phone lit up with his text message: "I'm parked out front. You ready?"

At the club, when Ben asked about Charlie, I mostly brushed it off. It was so loud that we couldn't hear each other over the music, and he took my face in his hand and drew me closer so he could talk quietly into my ear. It was electric. All night we talked like that, leaning close, noses touching ears as if we were telling secrets. My heart never stopped racing, not for a second.

"I'm glad you came with me. This would've been terrible without you here," he said.

Then I saw Charlie walk in, tall and undeniably handsome with a two-week-old beard.

"I'm so sorry," I said, "but I have to go." I was crestfallen.

Ben followed my eyes across the room to Charlie and stood up from the booth to let me out. I could always sense there was something missing with Charlie. Though everything about him screamed "perfect," there was a stilted cadence to our conversations. That's what I liked about Ben—his rough edges. Which made him perfect.

All night, I was watching for Ben out of the corner of my eye. I saw him in the crowd, breaking up a fight his friends had gotten into. I loved that he was not the kind of guy who used his formidable size to start fights but the kind who used it to end them.

I couldn't protest, nor did I want to. Charlie must've known he was done for, but he was a good sport. "All right," he said. "Well, y'all be careful. I'll call you later, Erin." Twenty-four hours later, Charlie would be in my rearview.

We got into Ben's car, his rowdy friends in the back, and as we pulled onto the highway Ben reached across the armrest and took my hand. I felt his warm hand curl around mine, so aware of the way it felt, his rough thumb rubbing the top of my knuckles. It felt impossible and electric.

By 4 a.m., after dropping the last person off, we headed back into town for Ben to get a peach Nehi before calling it a night. He went into the store, came back out, opened the drink, and took a

It was short and innocent, like a kiss at the altar on your wedding day. The sweetest kiss I'd ever had.

At closing time we were all herded outside. When we stepped into the night air, Ben was bombarded by drunk friends needing rides home, and he got to work arranging a ride for each of them. I admired the ease with which he did so, the way everyone listened, the fact that it was clear he did it all the time. His friends slumped into cars as Charlie came up behind me.

"Hey, I can drive you home if you need me to," Charlie said.

Ben turned and put his hand on my lower back to ease me toward his car.

"I brought you here," he said, "and I'll take you home."

sip. Then he turned to me. "Would it be all right if I kissed you?" he asked.

"You can't ask something like that!" I said, emboldened by my sleepiness. "You have to just do it."

He nodded, as if pondering that to himself. On the way back to campus, he stopped at the four-way intersection between the florist and the snow cone stand, turned my face toward his, and tilted my lips up to his own. It was short and innocent, like a kiss at the altar on your wedding day. The sweetest kiss I'd ever had.

Ben

DECEMBER 10, 2004

The next night Erin and I planned to look at Christmas lights around Laurel, mostly as an excuse to ride around and talk. She pulled up outside my house in her Beetle, and I came around to the driver's side.

"I'll be driving your car tonight, ma'am," I told her.

We hugged as she came out to go around to the passenger side.

When I got in, I adjusted the driver's seat, leaned across the armrest, and kissed her lips, which tasted like crème brûlée. Inside the car, it was as though I were swimming in her; the smell of her perfume was all around me.

We spent the night driving all over Laurel. I didn't care about the location; we could've been anywhere. I would've been happy to spend the rest of my life in that little blue Bug, staring at her green eyes, bathing in her smell, the sound of Damien Rice's peaking falsetto, and her sweet voice, talking about nothing and everything. We were headed together fast, plunging into something real and scary and forever. But it felt so easy.

Erin

DECEMBER 11, 2004

People say my daddy is as tough as a lightered knot, and they are right. A former college football star who looks like Harrison Ford, he has an intimidating way of making even arrogant people shrink in his presence. I was worried what Daddy would think of Ben's beat-up old car, his shaggy hair, his happy-go-lucky attitude. He had never, ever approved of any boyfriend of mine, deeming them all "sorry," so I felt a bit anxious when Ben

started angling to meet him. He was up for the challenge.

I got out of work at the hospital pharmacy the next night to find Ben waiting for me in the parking lot, leaning against my car. Winter weather had returned, and my mom had asked me to pick up Christmas wrapping paper before going to their house after work.

When we walked into my house, Daddy was in his spot on the sofa, watching TV. Ben said hello to my mother—whom he had already met—and made a beeline right for him. "Hey, Dr. Rasberry, Ben Napier. Good to meet you."

My five-foot, seven-inch daddy took in all six feet, six inches of Ben, gave him a firm handshake.

Ben invited himself to sit on the sofa, opposite Daddy.

"What are we watching here?" he asked. I loved that he said "we," as though he'd been there all evening. It was so natural and easy, as though he was giving Daddy no choice but to like him. "The History Channel? We don't get this on campus. I love the History Channel." He wasn't just saying that: he really did love the History Channel.

Ben could not have realized it, but he was boldly walking into the lion's den. Daddy is a lovable man, but he's a daunting presence, especially at first blush. He's also an expert on American history, especially the Civil War, even taking my mom on a two-week trip to visit every battlefield between Mississippi and Gettysburg. He's an ancestry buff, an avid reader of Shelby Foote and Ernest Hemingway, and a deep-sea fisherman to boot.

They watched, first in silence, and then they both started opening up. Daddy began baiting Ben, testing him in that sly way only a father of a daughter can do. He quizzed Ben on the order of US presidents being discussed in the show, feigning memory loss.

"No sir, Jackson was after the second Adams, and Van Buren was after Jackson," Ben pointed out. When Daddy flashed him a look of mild surprise, Ben added, "Wayne Academy taught us the song about the presidents."

Daddy was impressed, something he rarely is. He even liked Ben's shaggy hair, later saying it reminded him of how he'd worn it when he was in college.

Ben

DECEMBER 13, 2004

It took three days for me to know I was in love with Erin, but I didn't want to say it aloud and sound ridiculous. So I gave it three more days, which somehow seemed less ridiculous. I had never been in love with a girl, but it's funny: that's exactly how I knew I was.

"I think I've fallen in love with you," I said.

"I think I've fallen in love with you, too," she told me.

"One day I'm going to marry you," I said. "I'm sure about that." And I was. As sure as the rising sun and gravity and the order of the US presidents.

Erin

My plan had been to transfer to the Savannah College of Art and Design at the end of that second year. I had already accepted a scholarship, chosen my dorm, and met my advisers. But I had been having serious doubts, hesitant about the cost and sad at the thought of being a day's drive from Ben and my family. Ben had even been throwing around the idea of ditching Ole Miss and applying to schools in Georgia to be near me, which seemed crazy.

Suddenly my plan felt so arbitrary. I couldn't remember exactly why I'd wanted so badly to go to SCAD in the first place. By then I knew in my gut that my ability would matter more than my pedigree and the school name on my diploma.

"If you need to go to SCAD to get the best job, we'll pay for it," Daddy told me. "But if there is any way you'd think about Ole Miss, it sure would be good. You know, I loved it there. And Ben is going to Ole Miss. It wouldn't be so bad to spend a couple years up in Oxford with him, would it?"

I hadn't yet told Daddy, but I was already way ahead of him.

Ben

Having Erin in my life gave me some direction, a reason to keep my eyes front. After two years of mostly socializing at Jones, I started steering right at Ole Miss and actually enjoyed how it felt. My plan was straightforward and relatively simple: I was focused on finishing college with a decent enough GPA to get into graduate school, marry Erin, and teach history at a college. In Oxford I came to love my classes, especially in history and English. My focus was helped along by Erin's dad's ultimatum that I finish college before I could marry his daughter. That was as much motivation as a man needs. On top of that, I felt I had to be good enough to marry Erin. That's been my life since meeting her, striving to be good enough for her. I'd be lying if I didn't say it was hard as hell, but I feel as though it ought to be. Anything worthwhile is.

TOP: One week after meeting, the first photo of us together as a couple
in the yearbook room at JCJC, December 14, 2004.
BOTTOM: December 16, 2004, a week after meeting, the day before Ben left for a month for Christmas break.

Erin

At Ole Miss, Greek student life was everything, but neither Ben nor I, juniors and transfer students to boot, had any interest in that world. Once we found our people, strangers who became roommates and then friends, we began to feel as though we belonged. Ben became friendly, then

roommates, then inseparable with my high school friend Josh. My best friend at Ole Miss was Mallorie, a dairy farmer's daughter on an accounting scholarship. She was a country girl with ambition, never too proud or precious to get her hands dirty, but also a lady in every sense of the word. The day we met, I offered to highlight her hair, because I was "very good at it, trust me!" Though she walked out Marilyn Monroe platinum, she smiled and lied that it looked good. After she'd had a chance to go to the salon to fix my fiasco, we went antiques shopping in Oxford and became attached. Mallo-

rie was genuine without having to try to be, hospitable without an agenda, kind and generous in a way I wished the rest of the world would even try for. Her unaffected country girl sensibility reminded me of my mother; it comforted me and made her feel like family from the beginning.

I was young and finding my footing in an art school where I was a transfer student and, in my mind, an underdog. I was enamored with the way it felt walking through the heat of the kilns into the pottery studio. I liked the way it felt to pull ink across a screen evenly in the printmaking studio late at night.

Even back then, Ben and I were no good at being apart. We would spend all of our free time—and some of our not-free time—together. Ben would always come to my studio courses before they were over and watch me work and keep me company. On breaks we ate plate lunches from the four-corners Chevron or supper at Ajax. We'd spend Friday nights at Square Books, going upstairs and finding a quiet corner to read books we couldn't afford to buy.

We'd spend an hour on the comfortably worn armchairs and sofas and talk, listening to the sound of the skittering leaves on the porch of the Croft Institute overlooking the Grove, Ole Miss's giant lawn that is crazy on football Saturdays but a quiet refuge during the week.

LEFT: July 4, 2007, fireworks at Ole Miss. | RIGHT: Erin's twenty-first birthday in Memphis with Rebecca and Mallorie.

Art Major

At Ole Miss, my fine-arts education kicked into high gear as I began courses such as advanced graphic design, typography, printmaking, and advertising design—but most surprising to me was how much I enjoyed figure drawing. I became so much more confident in my sketching and journaling as I learned the curvature of the human spine and proportionate sizes of features on the human head. Ben even stepped in one day as the (fully clothed) figure model when the usual model couldn't make it while Ben was waiting for me outside my class. He became known as an honorary art student since he was always in the department with me after hours.

Scans from Erin's sketch pad 2005–2007, pencil, charcoal, and coffee.

In the late fall, I would pull my sweater tight around me, walking under his arm through the quad, where we would go our separate ways at Bondurant and Bishop, he to the English department, me to the journalism building. An hour later, he'd find his way to my desk and wait for me to finish up for the day.

Ben

Growing up, my mom was very crafty and encouraged it in us, asking us not to buy things, but to make her things on special occasions. At Valentine's, she would make our cards that we gave out in school. These might have been frugal decisions, but they were always cooler and more clever than the store-bought ones, and I guess some of it rubbed off on me.

In asking Erin to marry me, the proposal would have to be something special. It would have to be a big enough production to be worthy of our love story, like something out of movie or a book. I decided to take that idea for inspiration and run with it.

Erin and I spent many date nights perusing the bookshelves at Square Books and having a coffee on the balcony. For weeks I had been laying the groundwork for how I was going to propose.

Erin had taken a bookmaking course, and while

I didn't know the finer points, I had learned how to make a simple little book just from watching her. For weeks, I had been making a book for her, writing a story about a boy and a girl who no one thought matched but who fell in love fast in college.

The week before, I made the monthly trek with her down to Laurel, because it was time to have the conversation with her dad. Filled with the confidence of knowing what his answer would be, I breezed into his office at the hospital.

For some reason, though, when I was across from him, my self-assurance vanished. I knew her father well by then, and he knew me; we both knew the answer to the question, but for some reason, I felt panic rising up in me.

"Sit down, Ben!" Dr. Phil said jovially. "What're you doing in town?"

My voice was a little shaky as I cut right to it. "Well, I'd like your permission to ask Erin to marry me next Friday, the twenty-first."

The smile on his face faded into a kind of grimace and he took a beat. "That seems soon, don't you think, Ben?"

I was caught off guard. I began to sweat and just let my mouth run, not so eloquently. "Well, we've been dating for a few years now, and . . . and . . . and

TOP: Erin in the printmaking studio at the Ole Miss art school. | BOTTOM: Ben in the woodshop at the Ole Miss art school. This is where he first learned woodworking, waiting late nights on Erin to finish her studio work.

I love her very much, and . . . and . . . well, when do you think I should propose?"

My hands began to shake, and Phil leaned forward in his chair.

"Let me get this straight, Ben. You're wanting to marry Erin next Friday? What's going on?"

It was as though someone had given me oxygen. He had misunderstood the question, which was a relief. I explained that, with his permission, I would be proposing on the twenty-first. I guess I had dangled a modifier.

"Oh!" he said, laughing, relieved as well. "Oh, yeah, I think that'd be just fine."

Before I headed back to Oxford, I wanted to have a conversation with Erin's mammaw, with whom she was extremely close. Mammaw never had any daughters, and Erin is her only granddaughter. Very early in our relationship, we were having lunch at Mammaw's when she pointed at Erin and said, "That's my girl." I knew she meant it,

and it was important that I speak with her before proposing.

In the weeks prior I had asked my and Erin's moms and my grandparents about how their proposals had gone down. All were pretty straightforward. While we were talking that day, I asked Mammaw how her husband had proposed. Turns out that James Rasberry had asked with a bit more style. She told me, "He slid a little box across the table and said, 'I got something for you, Ouida.'"

Early that Friday morning, I went over to Square Books, set up pictures I'd had printed and flowers in big canning jars all over the balcony. They were on the tables, on the walls, on the rail, and on the columns.

Later I told Erin that I needed to go pick up a book for school, and our friends all found reasons to tag along. The hook was set; I gave Erin's roommate the book, her boyfriend was ready with a video camera, and I headed upstairs to the balcony.

LEFT: The Ole Miss campus inspired creativity around every turn.
RIGHT: Square Books was our favorite place in Oxford. It had to be the place Ben would finally propose.

The Square was full of people that day, in town for the Ole Miss versus Florida game. I waited anxiously. It was hot, without much of a breeze. Beads of sweat were beginning to form on my brow when she came through the door. I tried to hold back tears as I spoke to her.

My emotions got the best of me, and I had to whisper to keep from crying. "You know I'll always love you," I told her, "and that I'll always take care of you. In the words of James Rasberry, I got something for you."

She was crying and kept asking quietly, "What? What!"

I knelt down on one knee. "Will you marry me?"

She cried. "YES!" she gasped. "Yes, I will marry you!"

People below us in the Square were looking up, taking pictures, telling people on the phone what was happening, cheering for us. It was an auspicious beginning, I thought.

ABOVE: The first book I ever made for Erin and the antique ring box that held her engagement ring.

"I got something for you."

The proposal at Square Books in Oxford, Mississippi, on September 21, 2007.

Central Avenue today. The way we all wished it could be when we came home from college.

4

A Hometown

Erin

When I left for college, I saw only the problems with where I came from.

I had spent years feeling like an outcast, an orange in a crate full of apples. It had colored how I felt about myself, about my town, about the world beyond it. I had worn blinders much of the time that had kept me from appreciating what was there, what made this part of America special. Once I had been on my own long enough and had visited California, New York, and Europe, those judgments fell away.

As a jaded teenager, I'd dreamed of graduate schools and jobs in bigger cities, maybe Birmingham or Memphis. I'd felt my ambitions were bigger than Laurel, a small town where weeds sprang up in the sidewalk cracks, where the sour stench of the Masonite plant was always blowing in, where feral cats licked their paws in the broken windows of shuttered storefronts, where the graffiti in the alleys wasn't even good enough to give them character.

Downtown Laurel had lost its shine when I was a teenager, and I was foolish and young. I believed I could find what I was looking for—creativity, beauty, mystery—only somewhere else, somewhere with more concrete, more noise, and more people.

But I spent a summer of college interning at an ad agency in Memphis, and though I loved the work—and the rush of being part of a creative team—I was alienated by the ways of the big city. Its cuss words were too sharp for my small-town heart, its anonymity a little cold and empty. The city somehow resisted me. I never felt at home; I was not made for lonely meals and traffic noise, parking garages and overpasses, and having to worry about the New Madrid fault line opening up and swallowing me whole. Most of all, I did not like how hard it was to get home to visit my parents, who were three hundred miles away.

Laurel at its worst

Downtown Laurel was mostly shuttered when I was in high school and college.

I missed the easy quiet of Oxford and Laurel, the only other places I'd ever lived in. That summer, away from Ben, I also learned that I am not made to be alone, that I am my best when he is close by. Living in a big city after meeting Ben was like seeing an old friend and just not clicking with her in the way I'd used to. I began to realize that steady, faithful, wholesome Ben was the love of my life, and the embodiment of the very thing that I had been missing: home. He was the catalyst that made me want to return to Laurel, to embrace my roots, to recognize that I was my best when I felt connected, supported, and loved. As it came time for Ben and me to decide where we wanted to build a life, there was really no other choice.

I started to feel the magnetic pull to be with my people again. Ben and I could've started our lives anywhere, but only one place was close to our support system. I missed my dad singing Conway Twitty songs, my mama reading her newest columns for the newspaper out loud while we ate dinner. I missed the Main Street Festival every fall, the simple pleasure of eating a melty cheese-on-a-stick from the Corn Dog 7 at the Sawmill Square Mall.

Laurel was not somewhere to run away from but a place that would always welcome me back with open arms. And eventually, on visits home, I began to see something else: I saw magic and possibility. I started to see Laurel's empty storefronts not as failings but rather as rich, black soil. I knew about the turn-of-the-century architecture hidden underneath the ugly facade of urban renewal. As I walked past, ignoring the cracked glass, the 1980s signage of a long-defunct insurance office, I imagined *The Shop Around the Corner* coming to life in there. I envisioned a bookstore with checkerboard floors and oak shelves, or a little shop where I could buy fancy soaps or pretty pajamas, a toy store where a model train might run around the perimeter.

LEFT: Lauren Rogers Museum of Art at sunrise. | RIGHT: The alley beside the Presbyterian church.

Walking Laurel

The black line marks our favorite walking path through the historic district, past shopping and eating downtown in the red area, then north up 5th Avenue to see the largest residential historic district in Mississippi. The smell of sweet olive is everywhere on this walk in the spring and fall.

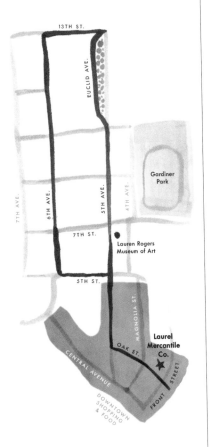

The charming, sweet idiosyncrasies of my town—what it was and what it could be—reminded me that I didn't need to be in a big city with millions of people; I just needed to be surrounded by things and people and places that inspired me.

Laurel people are a curious, mixed-up lot. There are the gritty manual laborers, the backbones of the factories; you'll find them hollering for the high school football team on Friday nights or the next morning, dressed in camouflage, high up in a tree stand. There are the high-culture families of generational wealth, whose forebears built the town or were donors to the art museum and who have country homes in North Carolina. There are the young mothers, military wives, and teachers whose towheaded babies wear smocked rompers and pink bows the size of bread loaves. There are the creatives making prints from woodblocks and watercolors, doctors who live in the newer neighborhoods outside town and give hell to the oilfield guys at church about the weekend's college football matchup. There are neighbors who deliver hot pound cakes to the doorsteps of the sick or those new in town. There are the thirty-year-old Oldsmobiles with twenty-inch rims thumping past the car wash and the Land Cruisers plastered with decals from trips to Nantucket, Sewanee, and the Appalachian Trail.

Even with our surface differences, Laurel is a community of people who care deeply for one another; our stark differences complement one another. It's what makes this place different from your place. That's the mystery and magic about it. I just hadn't seen it when I was younger.

A lot of it came about because of the walks.

Since Ben and I had met, we'd been taking walks around Laurel, seeing the town on foot, picking out which houses would be our dream homes. When we moved here, those afternoon walks became a ritual, and I soon fell in love with all of it: the shaded cobblestone alley beside the Presbyterian church that reminds me of the Old North Church in Boston; the Japanese magnolias that bloom in winter, always before we're expecting them; two poured-concrete mansions the color of peaches and cream with green tile roofs that

could have been clipped from a Spanish architectural magazine; Gardiner Park and its lantern lights that buzz to life at dusk.

Even though I'd driven past those places my entire life, seeing them on foot changed my perspective. The cross streets and houses that had once been just way-finding landmarks, now stood tall as inspiration and stories of the past. Flat pictures through car windows transformed into a landscape in all its three-dimensional glory, alive and buzzing. On our walks, I saw my city under a micro lens: the oddities of each block, the yard gnome and the bright yellow ginkgo tree, the red front door and the woman in the wide-brimmed hat who walked her black dog each afternoon. They became characters in our new life.

Our path was always the same: First we walked past our church with its copper steeple and front lawn, the grass spotted and bare in places from the pumpkin patch every October. Then north on 5th Avenue, where we passed one of the best art museums in the South and the first in Mississippi, Lauren Rogers Museum of Art. It held curiosities that had cast a spell on me in grade school: the world's second-smallest woven basket displayed under a magnifying glass, no larger than a speck of pepper; a suit of armor in the study that smelled like old books and furniture polish; a Rembrandt self-portrait—just a tiny black-and-white print; a Mary Cassatt portrait of a woman bathing; a Winslow Homer painting of a woman with her back to us walking toward the sea; an Alice Neel portrait of a slew-footed young girl in a floppy hat and red swimsuit standing defiantly on a beach; Andy Warhol's Jersey cow in fluorescent purple and pink.

Then Ben and I would turn on 6th Avenue and 7th Street, down the best-preserved street of classic homes in the city. Their histories are more like folklore: the ghosts that haunt the kitchen of an apartment that was once the first doctor's office in town, the tiny eight-by-twenty-foot house between mansions built as a pigeon's roost for an eccentric pharmacist. We'd pass the McLeods' home, where Mr. Roger is often busy on a ladder keeping the siding shipshape, scraping and repainting every inch the family's favorite shade of sky blue. We'd see him pouring sand onto a bare spot on the lawn, restoring every flaw each new season brings. In his youth he once rode a motorcycle down from New York wearing his entire wardrobe, shedding layers as the temperature rose—he must've been nearly naked when he made it to Mississippi.

We passed the Craftsman home where James Street grew up before he wrote *Tap Roots* and *Good-bye, My Lady*, the two Queen Annes built across 8th Street from each other for Lula and Ella, two sisters who'd lived next to each other all their lives. Each house had a grand front porch, turrets, and dormers with trim that remind me of gingerbread houses.

As we reached the bottom of the hill at 6th Avenue and 10th Street, a Foursquare-style home, sturdy and beautiful, would reveal itself in all its

ABOVE: Laurel is most photogenic at the corner of 5th Avenue and 7th Street.

glory. No matter how many times I saw it, its lime-washed brick and the gas lanterns flickering and glowing on the deep front porch never failed to bring my breath up short. I would imagine myself living there, among the squares of light cast through its million windows, my bare feet on the polished hardwood floors, the smell of seafood gumbo with a single bay leaf drifting up from the kitchen.

At the end of 6th Avenue, we'd turn right onto 13th Street and pass the cozy hobbit cottage of a printmaker, whose work I could see all over the walls through the living room window. Then another right onto Euclid Avenue, a long, narrow neighborhood that runs parallel to Euclid Park and a stream shaded by towering magnolia trees. I'd imagine the cheeky grandmother who'd placed the garden gnome inside the hollow base of one of the oaks that Ben and I had found and named Saul.

Inside Euclid Park, Ben once found a Laurel brick half buried in the dirt. Laurel bricks were once made in a now defunct local factory and are prized for their connection to Laurel's roots. Those of us born and raised here place Laurel bricks in the floors, driveways, fireplaces, and foundations of our homes for good luck. The one at my parents' house was placed squarely in the center of the brick

front porch when it was built in 1992, an engraved welcome that reminded me of a fossil when I was young.

At the end of Euclid, we would carry on back down 5th Avenue and past the grandest turn-of-the-century estates in the city. Those homes belonged to the original founders who settled Laurel in 1882. Sweet Olive, a cream Mediterranean, is my favorite of the 5th Avenue mansions for its uniquely formal European details that were so alien to a girl raised in the country. Towering sweet olive bushes grow all around it, their intoxicating sweet citrus smell acting as Laurel's signature perfume in the spring and autumn. I've heard there's a ballroom in the house, and I like to imagine the Reeders having Christmas Eve parties and dancing to Ella Fitzgerald, the smell of bergamot and apple cider permeating the room.

Next, we'd pass the Lindseys' shingled home, enormous and classically American, with a second-story porch that invites a summer nap in the rain. In that house, the world-renowned opera singer Leontyne Price found her first audience as a young girl. Her aunt worked for the Chisholm family, who lived there, and they used their connections to help send her on her way to the Metropolitan Opera. Every year they host wine-tasting parties for the Episcopal church, stringing lights across their polo field of a backyard beside the swimming pool. During the parties you can hear music on the wind, smell the beef bourguignon cooked in bacon grease and red wine, and see a faint glow above the tall privacy hedges. I always feel delighted by it, imagining Nick Carraway and Mr. Gatsby clinking wineglasses under those lights.

ABOVE: Euclid Avenue.

Laurel these days

Downtown Laurel nowadays on Thursday nights in the summer.

A HOMETOWN 49

a ride around town in the old Chevy

As we passed the museum again, we'd walk beneath the outstretched arms of monstrous live oaks on our way home. At that point we usually found we were starving, so more often than not, we'd stop at Lee's Coffee & Tea for our favorite meal: a brisket sandwich for Ben, French onion soup thick with roast beef for me.

At one table, we'd almost always spot Mr. George, who reminds me of a thin Santa Claus in a chambray button-down neatly tucked into khaki shorts and white tennis shoes. Every morning he'd come in at 8 a.m. with his briefcase and cane, writing until noon, when he'd take a nap in a chair on the second-story mezzanine. He'd pack up at 3 p.m. and make the slow, careful walk back home to his yellow apartment on 5th Avenue. He published a best-selling novel in 1977, traveled the world as a magazine correspondent, and lived in Manhattan and Rome before coming back home to Laurel. When I was growing up, he was a fixture at the first coffee shop in town where I played music on Thursday nights.

Mr. George became a grandfatherly figure to me, writing stories about my shows for the local newspaper and sending me a high school graduation card with a twenty-dollar bill inside. When that coffee shop closed, he migrated to Lee's, where he continued to write and watch. If he did not arrive by 8:15 a.m., the girls at the café, his watchful caretakers, would send someone to check on him.

As Thoreau wrote, "Half the walk is but retracing our steps," and I take comfort from that, knowing it is not just a literal statement. To return from where we left, we are retracing our steps, but in moving forward in life, I think we are also trying to rediscover the things that made us innocent, hopeful, and free. The things that are harder to find as we age. Those walks put me inside that feeling, and I tried to rediscover parts of myself on each one. The walk itself, the one Ben and I ritualized, was its own editing exercise: the path we chose, what we decided to look at, the details we took in, the selves we decided to be.

When we are young, we take chances. We consider briefly that something might go badly, but maybe it won't. So we plow ahead, betting on our instincts, faulty as they may be. It might look as if those of us from small towns who move back home are making a safe bet or no bet at all. But I disagree: it takes effort to rediscover what you think you already know, and there's an unsung bravery at work. We may find nothing. Or, if we shift our perspectives, we allow for the possibility that life can crack open with wonder and we can find magic in the familiar.

Or, if we shift our perspectives, we allow for the possibility that life can crack open with WONDER and we can find MAGIC in the familiar.

The day my parents got another son and I became a Napier. I love that Mallorie and Ben's daddy are in this photo, each giving their blessing.

Photo by Patrick Little

5

A Vow

Erin

In the lavish, cream-colored bride's room at the church where I would soon walk down the aisle to become a wife, I was shaking.

It was the coldest November day Oxford, Mississippi, had seen in decades, and inside Paris-Yates Chapel at Ole Miss both the broken heater and my nerves were having their way with me. I was not at all nervous about marrying Ben; that was the one thing that I felt completely at ease with. The anxiety came from everything else: being the center of attention, making this formal declaration of independence and adulthood, holding the day permanently in my mind's eye. I wanted to remember every moment of this day that would pass too quickly, to create mental photographs, to commit each detail to memory so I could relive it whenever I wanted to.

Slipping out of my white button-down and blue jeans, I stepped into my sleeveless antique white lace gown. My cousin Kelsa, my maid of honor, had carefully curled my hair and applied my makeup earlier, finishing the look with an antique birdcage veil. Mama fastened a thousand buttons up the back of my dress and, to keep me warm before the ceremony, pulled her white wool coat over my shoulders. Mallorie tied the champagne-colored sash—heavy with pearls and

ABOVE: Leaving the bride's suite, about to walk down the aisle. *Photo by Brooke Davis*

jewels—around my waist with a crisp bow at the small of my back. Hidden at the bottom of the heavy, long layers of lace and silk were satin high heels the color of the sky, a jeweled brooch at each toe. Tied around my bouquet was my grandmother's heart-shaped locket, and inside were photos of my grandparents, three of whom had passed on and Mammaw, who was too frail to travel.

For four years Ben and I had shared a love and commitment to each other that had only grown stronger. With each passing day, we were a knot being pulled tighter. We had shared our deepest secrets and fears, desires and dreams. Now we would take what was already in our hearts and make it official in the presence of God and our loved ones; we would formalize our union to the world.

Under the arched doorways of the atrium, Daddy and I waited alone. When I looked over at him, I saw the restrained emotion on his steely face. He kissed my cheek, and I held back tears as my mind flashed to a home video: Daddy smiling in a white undershirt, holding a six-month-old with sleepy eyes, while he swayed and quietly sang about how he had sunshine on a cloudy day.

Neither of us said it, but I knew he felt it, too, the resonance of what was about to happen, the symbolic transfer: he was about to give me away to the boy we had both come to love. That feeling was in the room with us, weighty and poignant; the power of what can pass between a father and a daughter without words.

Ben

Even with two hundred warm bodies present it was still brisk in that chapel, which thankfully kept me from sweating beneath my three-piece suit. Fortunately we'd nixed the idea, floated by my brothers, of wearing kilts, a nod to my Scottish heritage. In the preceding months Erin and my dad had planned every detail of our formal church service together, from the aesthetic to the theological, from "Welcome" to "You may kiss the bride." It was important to all of us that the service have meaning and weight, instead of just being a ten-minute prelude to a party. We wanted it to touch on the universal and the personal, the communal and the individual. It was about the special connection between Erin and me as well as the bond that holds us all together, the moment when we would become one.

Whether or not I would cry was not even a question; instead there was a running bet among the groomsmen as to when it would happen. I waited with my three brothers, Erin's brother, my dad, and two of my best friends to take our places like a basketball team waiting to run onto the court. As we walked from the atrium to the altar, I felt the gravity of what we were doing, the sense of mission.

Bagpipes pierced the silence, and then the crowd stood and turned. Erin stepped through the door.

ABOVE: Daddy, just before he gave me away. *Photo by Patrick Little*

TOP: Ben is more tenderhearted than you might expect. | BOTTOM LEFT: Paris-Yates Chapel.
BOTTOM RIGHT: I carried my grandparents with me. *Photos by Patrick Little*

Daddy caught my eyes and asked quietly in his slow, thick voice, "Are you ready?"

His voice has always made me feel safe. It's gentle but gravelly, measured and sure, and it fills a room whether he's preaching to a congregation, telling a story at dinner, or telling one of his boys to bring him something. It gives a sense of peace and gentleness.

"Yes, sir," I answered.

So he began: "I, Ben, take you, Erin."

I breathed in. But when I opened my mouth, I couldn't speak.

Erin

Daddy and I walked down the aisle, and I felt like a plucked goose, shivering with nerves and the cold until I reached Mama and Ben's mom at the front. Our brothers flanked Ben's daddy, who was wearing his somber black robe and white satin stole, waiting for us at the altar. And there stood Ben.

Ben had pulled me back into the kind of faith I had resisted for some years. He had showed me his faith, which was about grace and love and practicing those things methodically—an approach that was totally foreign to me. With Ben, faith felt a lot like freedom from the things that scared me, rather than an obstacle to what I loved. I found comfort in it—and in him for leading me to it. Faith was such an integral part of who he was. And I was drawn to it.

Ben

When we began our vows, everything in that church went silent, including my mind. It was just Erin and me standing up there alone in front of my dad, solid and steady as a diesel engine. A mountain of a man.

Erin

Ben's eyes brimmed with tears and his cheeks glowed pink, with a kind of Santa Claus warmth. He took a beat, struggling to speak, and I squeezed his hands. "It's okay," his dad whispered in his warm voice. "I know this is big, but it's okay. Take your time."

Ben's brother Tom and I met eyes and shared a knowing smile; Ben had always been the tender-hearted brother. After some quiet and a nervous laugh among the congregation, Ben laughed, too. And found his composure.

After the vows, I slipped a simple gold band onto his finger and he placed an antique-inspired diamond chip–encrusted white and rose gold ring on mine.

On our way out of the chapel, our friend Jessie, a bagpiper, played "Scotland the Brave." Departing the church, I felt the cold fall away, and I realized, for the first time, that I was walking on my husband's arm.

We took the city's British double-decker bus to our cozy party inside the old Oxford Train De-

ABOVE: Erin with her aunt Mae, her mom, Aunt Phyllis, and Aunt Charlotte before the wedding. *Photo by Brooke Davis*

Our wedding day, the way I remember it. *Photos by Patrick Little*

The Anniversary Books

Through the years, Ben has kept the tradition of the anniversary books, even if it means giving one months after the fact because life got so busy around our actual anniversary. He promised me that as long as I'm his girl, I'll get my book. I'd rather have these than anything else in the world.

pot. We danced late into the night to the Temptations, Elton John, and Louis Prima and ate salty ham biscuits, hot artichoke dip, and vanilla cupcakes, all washed down with glass-bottled Cokes. At the end of the night we stepped outside into the air redolent with fall, a distant bonfire, and burnt fuel: my grandfather's old Pontiac, passed down to Ben, sat idling for us. We drove off as our family and friends showered us with bright yellow ginkgo leaves, collected just that morning.

Ben

To say we were frugal in those first few years of marriage is an understatement. Even on our honeymoon in New York, we shared every meal, including the best steak I've ever tasted at Delmonico's. Paper is the traditional gift for the one-year anniversary, and it's common to give books or concert tickets or a Bible, but I wanted to do something unique, to set the tone for our singular love.

During our first year of marriage I secretly documented the things—big and small—that happened each month: struggles, breaks, losses, cars, dogs, dinner on a rooftop, a trip, lunch with an old friend, and whatever else I considered to be a moment worth remembering. I wrote a brief story for each month and included some sort of illustration: a photo Erin had taken or bad clip art that would make her laugh. Every month had a picture on the left-hand page and a story on the right.

The anniversary book was a way to give Erin something without breaking the bank. Though we celebrate our actual wedding anniversary, the week we met in college is more important to us. But Erin deserved something special to commemorate the day we became husband and wife. Leaning on my bookmaking experience, I bound it all together with a ticking fabric cover and titled it simply *Our 1st Year of Marriage*.

I didn't realize it then, but I set a high-water mark that I have to meet every time November rolls around. Every year, I struggle to fit the past year's events into my template, since there's always more I want to remember than space on the page. I guess that's a good problem to have, an embarrassment of riches. I use some of our personal photos and old ephemera to illustrate each month and end each entry with the three simple words: "I love you." The anniversary books are both

My favorite things

entirely worthless and completely invaluable to Erin. It's like the first pieces of furniture I ever made for her; though they're nothing compared to what I can build now, she'll never let me replace them.

Erin

The books are my most precious belongings. When the tornado sirens wail in the summer, I run to our bedroom and grab the books to take to safety. They are the tender records of our relationship, the most valuable thing I own.

The morning of our second anniversary, I woke up while it was still dark, having felt Ben leaving the room. (We call him "Big" for a reason—it's hard for him to do anything stealthily, and his heart matches his size.) I couldn't go back to sleep, as I was quietly anticipating what he might be up to. Hearing noises from our living room and knowing he could probably use some time, I stayed in bed and wrote him a letter, thinking about how he thrives off surprising me.

In college he would call me from his parents' house in north Mississippi to say he'd be back in five hours or so. Then, when I hung up, I'd hear a knock on my door, and there he would be smiling and scooping me up into his arms.

On our first Valentine's Day, he picked me up from work and took me to my parents', who were out of town. In their kitchen he cooked twenty grilled cheese sandwiches and ten pieces of raisin toast with apple butter, a huge pot of grits, an entire carton of eggs. He never explained why he had cooked so much for just the two of us, but we laughed until I cried. It was endearing that he cooked the way his mom did, for an army of men. It was just his instinct.

ABOVE: The proposal book, first year: paper, second year: cotton, third year: leather, fourth year: flowers, fifth year: wood, sixth year: iron, seventh year: wool and copper, eighth year: linen and bronze.

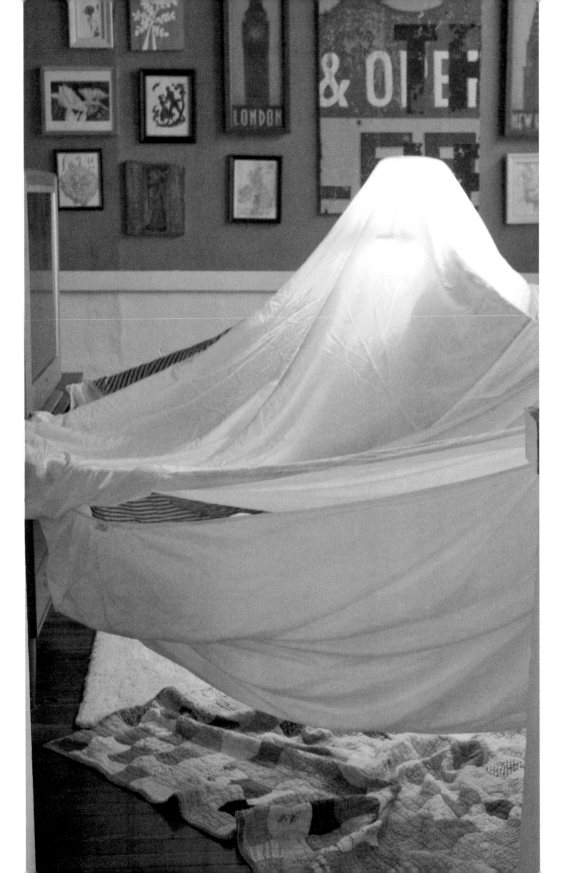

For my twentieth birthday, he couldn't afford to take me out to one of the nice restaurants on the Square in Oxford, so he grilled grocery store steaks at home with baked potatoes and asparagus, bundled them up in tinfoil, and picked me up for a surprise date. He took me to the Square, where there was a dinner table set up in the quiet alley beside the children's book store with candles and ginger ale. In that starlit square we unpacked and enjoyed our dinner, infinitely more than we would have at any restaurant.

On the morning of our second anniversary, I finished my letter, took a shower, and went into the living room to find a cozy tent made from mismatched bedsheets and patchwork quilts.

In a nod to one of our favorite movies, *The Holiday,* Ben had made a tent in our living room, and called it a "cotton house," to mark our second anniversary, for which the traditional gift is something made of cotton. I climbed inside to find him there, a giant with legs like sycamore trunks, surrounded by a pile of gifts, each wrapped in cotton. "A little more cotton for the sweetest girl in the world," the note read. "Thank you so much for the best two years of my life."

I pulled out a sweet cotton blouse, a cozy, woolly cardigan, and then Christmas cookie cutters from inside a cotton pillowcase. We had breakfast together, and then he dug around in the mountains of blankets and pillows to give me one last thing: a bouquet of cotton flowers in vintage fabrics, custom-made by our friend Dawn. She had used the fabrics on a pillow once, and I'd thought it was so lovely. Ben had remembered and asked her to use it to make me a bouquet of flowers—one that wouldn't, couldn't ever die.

Ben tries to give me the world, and sometimes that's the world as I wish it would be. It's one of the things I love so much about him. When he can't do that, he is able to make something good each day for me—which will always be more than enough.

FACING PAGE: The cotton house surprise on our second anniversary. | ABOVE LEFT: Reading the second anniversary book he made. ABOVE RIGHT: Flowers that will never die. This is a man who knows how to do romance.

6

A First Home

Ben

I've never really had a hometown.
Or, depending on how you want to look at it, I've had a lot of them.

As a Methodist preacher's kid, I called about six different small towns home before I became a married man. Home was always more a state of mind than anything else.

So I was excited to start a new life with Erin; putting down roots in Laurel, a place where she already had them, felt good to me. Actually, putting down roots anywhere felt good. It was as though I had been carrying something heavy for a long time, and I was relieved to finally lay it all down.

I fell in love with Erin's hometown while falling in love with her, so you could say that my love of Laurel was an extension of that love. And because she had come full circle about where she had grown up, we decided to build a life together here, in the place that had grown her.

Erin has long been motivated by the idea that a person, place, or thing can be what you want it to be—whether that is something you envision or remember or just want so badly that you can bring it to life. She had a desire for her hometown to be the idyllic place that her imagination conjured up from memories, one that loosely approximated city life: sprawling festivals, crowded restaurants, unique shopping. We decided that if we were going to be eight minutes from her parents' place in the country, we'd at least live as though we were in a big city, in a walk-up loft downtown. A place where Amtrak's Crescent Line, which went all the way to New York City, would shake plaster dust from our walls.

Erin's family owned a historic hundred-year-old flatiron building that we transformed into our first home. The space, the freedom, and the affordability made it easier for Erin to stomach the comments of friends who'd moved on to bigger cities and subtly took jabs at her choice of "settling." Until our wed-

FACING PAGE: Our first home was a loft we renovated in downtown Laurel, built in 1910.

TOP LEFT: The stairs we painted red when we moved in. | TOP RIGHT: We turned a doorway into a headboard.
BOTTOM: The living room where my old dresser became a TV console.

ding, for about ten months, we lived apart. She lived with her parents, while I lived in—and worked on renovating—our first home.

During those months, I had only a toilet, a sink, and a bed. By then, Erin's Ole Miss roommate, Mallorie, and her cousin Jim were engaged and renovating the loft in the building adjoining ours, which had the luxury of a fully functioning bathroom. At 6:30 every morning, I would wake up, start my coffee, get dressed, go downstairs to the sidewalk, walk to their door, go up to their apartment, shower, get dressed again, go back to our place, and wait for the contractors who dealt with the big-picture stuff such as the plumbing and wiring. It was like my own personal walk of shame, every day.

The two-story flatiron building in downtown Laurel had been Erin's uncle's former offices and a toothpaste factory after World War II. It was the shape of a pizza slice with a bite taken from the tip of the triangle and virtually no square-shaped rooms inside. On the ground floor there was a small insurance company, and the second floor was to be our loft. It was a beautiful, drafty old place.

Erin and I came up with a plan, made some drawings, and looked to execute it in a way that wouldn't bankrupt us. The dark and creaky plank floors had a hole the size of a half-dollar near the stove that once swallowed a drill bit I had dropped. The nine-foot-tall single-pane windows were a century old and would have cost a fortune to replace, so we learned to love how the wind whispered through them in the winter and how we felt like ants under a magnifying glass in the summer.

We cut costs everywhere we could, taking on DIY projects, painting, and coming up with affordable substitutes for certain finishes and details. When it came to furniture, we had a lot of hand-me-downs, and I took it upon myself to build a few pieces.

I had found carpentry almost by accident, or, I guess you could say, it had found me. At Ole Miss, a fair amount of my time was spent in the art department, waiting for Erin to finish her studio work. Soon enough, half bored, half curious, I wandered into the wood shop to kill time. I became friends with a couple of those guys, good ol' boys with manual labor experience who had discovered they had an inclination for art. They showed me some tricks with the planer and the table saw, and pretty soon, I got my basic start. I can do this, I thought.

The work came naturally to me in a way that nothing else had. I wouldn't even call it work; it never felt like it. I began with the simpler things: building picture frames for Erin's artwork along with the work of others she admired, which we hung all over the loft. Eventually, if Erin saw a piece of furniture she thought I could build, all she had to do was ask and I was game. It didn't occur to me at the time to make a life out of it; it was more like a skill I could use when needed.

The more I got into woodworking, the more I loved it. With every piece, I wanted to tell a story. The furniture had to be beautiful, but the story it told made it even more beautiful. I didn't want to build pieces that looked like a bunch of scrap thrown together. I wanted them to be detailed, thoughtfully designed, useful pieces of art. Backed by the confidence my father had passed down to me, I dived in, feeling around as I went.

I had nothing to look at or go off of, which is still how I do it to this day. As my mother did in the kitchen, I worked with what I had. Like my dad, I was fear-

Football Saturdays

I didn't care much about Ole Miss football while I was a student, but after I graduated, it felt like the right thing to get behind every Saturday in the fall. Erin's parents built a massive deck overlooking their backyard and lake when she came home from college, and it became hallowed ground for tailgating with

her whole family, with its huge TV, Rotel dip, and lots of grilled meat. Her dad would light a fire in the fire pit and play the Ole Miss band CD while we all played cornhole or watched old matchups on ESPN Classic to pregame. This tradition has become more important to us than I ever imagined it would. It's not so much about the game as it is about ritual, family, and being intentional about doing this together every weekend. Ole Miss doesn't always win, but as long as we're partying on Erin's parents' back porch, it doesn't dampen our spirits (much).

less about trying. With each piece I completed, the more I wanted to know about the craft. I learned about doing miter cuts, pin joints, mortise-and-tenon joints, breadboards on tables. While browsing an antiques store, Erin saw a rough-looking armoire painted blue, something from an early 1900s farmhouse. It was essentially a cabinet built around a six-panel door; at three grand, it was well out of our budget, so Erin took pictures and measured it and asked if I could build one and paint it white. I had no idea if I could.

"Of course I can," I said.

In order to build that armoire, I again looked to the past. Erin's grandfather—who had passed away when she was a teenager—had been an elected supervisor in the county, and when a building was being torn down, he'd save parts of it in his shop. The rafters in his workshop were full of old doors, and I found one that was perfect. It was the first time I'd built something with reclaimed materials that had personal meaning, which Erin and I would eventually make our signature way of working. Building a new armoire off of something from her grandfather's collection was the perfect distillation of what we were trying to do.

It was our first home, so I was careful and deliberate with each choice. We were building something—both literally and figuratively—and even when we left, its fingerprints would remain on us and ours on it. In every decision we made for the apartment, we were very aware that it would be our first home—with all the importance and symbolism that that meant.

We wanted our families and our history to be part of our home. I went on an excursion with Jim and my Ole Miss roommate Josh—who had recently married and was moving into the loft across the street—to salvage lumber from Erin's great-grandparents' home, and I built a few pieces from it.

TOP: The home office. | BOTTOM: The kitchen. It took me and Erin's dad an entire day to clean up the plaster dust that resulted from exposing the brick.

The walls of the loft were plaster and exposed brick. I put up pendant lights, tin backsplashes in the kitchen, some car parts for decorative art in my office. We painted the walls historic shades of cream and deep gray greens, the stairs a glossy red oil enamel. The plaster walls of the hallway and office were already stained the color of maple syrup and gave our apartment an autumnal feel year-round. Erin didn't mind it, and it was too expensive to change anyway, so we kept it.

Hardwood flooring was also too expensive, so we made the bathroom floors from durable beadboard paneling and painted it glossy white. Erin's mother found an old plaque inscribed "Napier Brothers Glasgow" with a brass British royal seal that we affixed beside the front door. I imagined that those brothers were some of my Scottish ancestors, who were once shipbuilders for the Royal Navy, a position that gave them the right to display the royal seal, which you could do only if you worked for the king or queen.

Every room had some tie to our family. In the guest bedroom we placed the metal bed that had belonged to Erin's grandparents when they were newlyweds. It was so small that we had to stretch it at a welding shop to fit a full-size mattress. I took the dresser that I'd had as a boy—a long midcentury modern piece with three stacks of drawers—and converted it into a console table. I refinished a table from Erin's dad's fishing camp, which became our dining room table, and recovered a set of metal chairs from my dad's garage in toile, which Erin felt feminized them just enough.

Even the little touches had some meaning. There was the bookshelf that my grandfather Ben Pickering had made for my mama, who had given it to me. In the office was the tailgate from my daddy's old '59 Ford. When I was a baby, my parents had had a drafty fireplace without a flue. Daddy had put a potbellied stove in front of it and sealed up the fireplace with a Phillips 66 sign, which he turned around and cut a hole out of for the stovepipe. It was more than just a cool old sign; it was a symbol of my dad's ingenuity, and I wanted it in our first home. So it became a piece of art. That's how we operate. We like those stories because they say something about where we came from. I think the whole point of life is that we're part of something bigger than ourselves. Feeling connected to our people and their stories makes them part of our own story. In a small way, it's a form of immortality.

While laying the foundation for our new lives in the loft, I turned outward as well. I had gotten a job as director of youth ministry at a church about forty-five minutes away and was still toying with grad school, but as much as I could, I made Laurel my life. Something about the town awoke a sleeping giant inside of me, one that I hadn't felt for a few years. Growing up, I'd watch my parents as we moved to a new small church in a new small town. They'd work within the church and the community to help bring a spark

ABOVE: My dad's old Phillips 66 sign.

TOP LEFT: Planting flowers in the first-floor flower boxes, 2010. | TOP RIGHT: Erin cooking summer squash.
BOTTOM LEFT: Erin's twenty-fifth birthday I made her a surprise breakfast and a card, 2010. | BOTTOM RIGHT: Flirting in the stairwell.

A sketch Erin did of the office and a Jane Austen quote.

back to the life there. I wanted to be a part of something like that.

As a nineteen-year-old at Jones, I did my best to make the campus a giant family. I wanted to turn the community college into a real community—and taking a page from Erin's book, I extracted what I could to make it happen. In Laurel, I wanted to do the same thing. The town wasn't exactly in its heyday when Erin and I arrived, and I wanted to bring a sense of community back to downtown, just as my parents had done in those small country churches, just as I had tried to do at Jones. There was one restaurant open for lunch during the week and one little coffee shop. The Southern Antiques Mall and a pageant dress shop were about the only places anyone would shop in downtown. The festivals either were smaller than Erin remembered or had been forgotten entirely. At first Erin was less than thrilled with Laurel's prospects, but together we began to see it as an opportunity. And we weren't the only ones wanting more out of this sleepy little town.

I was invited to be on the board of Laurel Main Street, a ragtag organization of building and business owners that worked on setting incentives and regulations to save the historic integrity of the downtown and bring in new businesses. It was part preservation and part economic development. As I saw it, Laurel already had the most important elements: thoughtful architecture, a deep and fascinating history, the largest and most intact residential historic district in all of Mississippi, and a once beautiful downtown, whose only problem was that the buildings were empty, the historic facades covered up by the cold aluminum mask of decades-old urban renewal.

The perception from the inside was that Laurel was a dying town, a stagnant relic of a once booming past. I didn't see it that way at all; it was beautiful, but it wasn't putting its best face forward. There was a defeatist attitude that permeated the town, a kind of communal and contagious giving up. Turning things around would be about changing perceptions and hearts. As a newcomer who saw what the town could be, I was excited to help the city return to its full glory in its residents' eyes. Erin also joined Laurel Main Street, and soon afterward, I was elected president, mostly because I already lived downtown.

Our mission was twofold: we wanted Laurel to be the way Erin remembered it, but at the same time, we wanted to bring a little big-city style and culture into it because we wanted to change the perception of living in a small town. We wanted others to realize that coming home wasn't settling but in fact represented a deep connection to your roots and a commitment to preserving the goodness of a small, tight-knit community.

Fortunately, we weren't starting from a standstill. Laurel has always maintained its industry, a feather in its hat for more than a century, so there are always new people moving here for work. The

> There was a defeatist attitude that permeated the town, a kind of communal and contagious giving up. Turning things around would be about changing perceptions and hearts.

industry that launched Laurel was the timber industry. In the early twentieth century, more board feet of yellow pine were milled in Laurel every day than anywhere else in the world. Once all the trees had been cut down, the town moved to the oil industry, which lasted until the recent oil price crash. Several companies sprang up to support those industries: transformer manufacturers, poultry producers, and others.

We also noticed that the louder we became about loving Laurel, the more it gave people the courage to do the same. It was almost as though they had just been waiting for permission to say it was a cool place to live. So many people in our community shared our vision and desires for the place; as we all organized our various gifts, the more Laurel became what it had always been capable of being.

One issue was that there was nowhere to eat downtown at night and consequently no reason to go there after sundown. If you wanted to eat out with your friends, you had to go to the chain restaurants by Interstate 59 or thirty miles south to Hattiesburg. There was a little park below our apartments, on the footprint of a previous building. Erin and I, along with Jim and Mallorie and Josh and Emily, started hosting potluck parties in the park. The idea was to create a city experience, friends and food under the stars downtown, surrounded by beautiful old buildings— a picture-perfect small-town gathering.

Erin was on the promotion committee of LMS and donated her free time by designing anything it needed: huge murals and signage, posters for the

ABOVE: The Loblolly Festival, where I would do my part as the town mascot.

Take me back home to the Free State of Jones

Supper club parties in the park below our apartment windows were always a big time. Cary Hudson came and played at this one in 2011.
Photos by Sam McAlister

festivals, stationery, a logo, brochures, and mail-outs. She was great at highlighting the things that already made Laurel great. I was on the committees that determined what public events and festivals would bring people downtown again. We rebooted and rebranded an old festival known as the Loblolly Festival, which has since become Laurel's biggest annual event; it celebrates our city's heritage as a lumber town, the world capital of loblolly pine, and

I became the mascot, the town lumberjack. When you're a strong, slightly overweight giant and can grow hair on your face as I can, anything less would be a waste of a God-given purpose. Things were starting to come together. We'd had a plan when we arrived, and we'd thought it would all play out a certain way. But of course, things never actually happen according to plan. Time moves on, things change, and so would we.

ABOVE: Mr. and Mrs. Loblolly in action.

TOP LEFT: A streetlight banner and ghost sign, both designed by Erin. | TOP RIGHT: The library mural she designed.
BOTTOM: The first mural she designed has become an iconic photo op in Laurel.

My first professional photo for my burgeoning business, taken in our kitchen.
It was still little more than a dream at that point.

Photo by Sam McAlister

7

Adrift

Erin

Like many twenty-somethings, Ben and I carried a bit of college with us into our adult lives.

We slept in on weekends, ate what we wanted, and lived our days as newly responsible adults while still trying to maintain the idealism and looseness of youth. College was prolonged for our little "framily"—the word I use to describe our tight-knit inner circle in Laurel.

My cousin Jim and Mallorie met at my senior art thesis and were newly married. They shared the firewall between our loft and the building next door. When we were young, Jim had always been kind to me, the only little girl in the family, and had made a point of including me in the boy fun. He was the one who would build forts with me at Mammaw's with tablecloths, rubber bands, and ladder-back dinner chairs. As neighbors in Laurel, Mallorie and I were as good as roommates, borrowing clothes from each other's closets and hosting supper parties in the park below our windows. Ben and Jim would string party lights into the oak trees and grill, while upstairs we made Mallorie's famous jambalaya, pigs in a blanket, or candied apples.

Across the street was the second-story patio of Josh, my childhood friend who had become Ben's roommate at Ole Miss, and his wife, Emily. They lived in a loft that reminded me of the apartment from *Ghost*, with expansive white walls and high ceilings. Josh was a good friend to Ben, even floating him on rent once in college before he found his footing with a job. He's always been generous beyond reason, having faith that the things he invests in, even a lovable burly roommate, will someday bear fruit. Emily became part of the framily a few years after college, and she filled the slot of the pragmatic one, wise beyond her years. In her twenties, she already knew the secret things our mamas knew after decades of experience:

1. If you wait long enough, it will go on sale.

2. From plumbing to taxes, if you pay attention, you can figure out how to do anything on your own.

3. Limes make pickles crunchy.

I relished the time we spent with the framily in our new homes, basking in the open future and holding tight to the idea that life is what you make it, that home is what you want it to be. Some days it took an effort to keep believing this. The reality was that time with my framily was a respite from the life I was actually living during the workweek.

It would start at 6 a.m. I'd shower and dress, leaving time to eat some Raisin Bran or toast with butter and strawberry jam. At 7:45, I'd get into my dented blue Beetle, crank it, and instinctively cringe as the same country song invariably sprang on:

Shift work,
tough work
for the busy convenience store clerk

For that fifteen-minute car ride, I would zone out until I pulled off the interstate. I'd pass through the winding landscaped corridor as the company's modern glass headquarters rose up from the middle of a vast field. There was not a single other building in sight in any direction, only grass and trees and parking lot.

Inside, I would pass through the sliding doors into the electric blue and orange lobby, swipe my badge, and take the stairs up one floor. I'd get out at the art department and follow the hallway to the electric blue walls of my six-by-eight-foot padded cubicle. My kingdom.

When I was young, I'd dreamed of a career in art, a calling in which I would create something meaningful and inspiring. I was drawn to the two-

ABOVE: The framily. Keeping college alive long after we had graduated. Emily, Ben, me, Josh, Mallorie, and Jim.

dimensional world of lettering and type, color and form, paint and paper, feeling and function. It felt like a kind of math where I enjoyed solving the problem (as opposed to actual math, which had always been a struggle). As I became more involved in the art world and expanded into new skills, my career path was clearly lit. It seemed that all I had to do was follow the lights.

But there was a problem. My pragmatic and loving parents, hardworking people raised by farmers and laborers who had turned Mississippi dirt into sugarcane and Silver Queen corn, were careful to manage my expectations: "It's going to be hard to have a job like that here, you know?" they would say.

And they were right.

So about six months after graduating and returning to Laurel, I took a position as a designer for a technology company. Grateful as I was for a steady job with benefits, it took a lot out of me. The corporate world can be a kind of punishment for those who relish creativity and a life at home.

By 8:05, I was in my adjustable chair, settling under the dull fluorescent lights, surrounded by concert posters and photos of Ben and me. One cubicle over was the second in command of our department, Sam, a talented designer and photographer. Over at the other wall was Shannon, a cool guy fresh out of design school who loved to talk college basketball. There was also James, in his thirties and very literary inside and out, the kind of guy I imagined letting loose at jam band concerts on the weekend. Jessica was tall with alabaster skin and a white-blond bob. She had thick black-rimmed glasses and drew anime at her desk during lunch.

Most people kept to themselves, in a fog, designing logos for products, lighting catalogs, and trade shows. At lunchtime, we would mill around the break area, surrounded by floor-to-ceiling glass. It was a little like standing on the edge of a bridge, as though you could jump and fly across the fields. Or I imagined I could.

We'd spend some days designing football magazines for the local high schools that the generous owners of our corporation supplied pro bono. I would labor over a booklet to make teenage players and cheerleaders look like professionals, though I sometimes found it a pleasant way to pass the hours. In my cubicle, I would wait for five o'clock, when I could finally get back to living for just a few hours until bedtime, before the cycle would start all over again. I was drained, stifled, creatively unsatisfied. I knew I was capable of more, knew I would thrive if I were only challenged and set free. I just didn't see how that was going to happen, sitting there surrounded by glass in a corridor off the interstate.

The answer came serendipitously and from an unlikely place. It was a type of salvation, though I didn't realize it at the time.

After college, I had started a blog to showcase my freelance design work of all kinds: branding, birthday party invitations, and our wedding stationery, which I had designed. Our invitations were nothing swirly or too ornamental, just two simple fonts that felt like me and Ben. The letterpress was hand printed on ivory cotton paper in red and blue inks that reminded me of the November colors of the trees and sky. The RSVP was a vintage postcard, a sepia-tone photograph of Oxford with a scalloped

Beach Days

In 1998, my parents bought a place down in Orange Beach, Alabama, and I spent much of my adolescence there, splitting my life between weekdays in Laurel and weekends diving below the surf, with the salty air tangling my half-dried hair, my legs the color of golden brown biscuits, my skin smelling permanently of Coppertone. Even when I finished college and was working in

the cubicle, it was a respite from real life: we'd make a run for it on a Friday night and come back home to Laurel on Sunday night, my overnight bag always carrying a trace of sand at the bottom.

edge, inspired by the postcards I'd found in Grandmother's hope chest.

My friend Annalee was really taken by my invitations and asked me to create a save-the-date for her wedding. She said, "Think outside the box, and don't worry about the budget at all." Being treated like a professional lit me up from the inside, and I got to work. I took ivory handkerchiefs with lace around the edges and screen printed the design in the center.

When I was finished, I snapped a photo of them to add to my blog—which I had named Lucky Luxe—packaged them in fancy boxes, and mailed them off. That was that. Until a few days later, sitting in my cubicle, I received an email from a woman in New York. She had come across my blog and absolutely loved what I'd done. She wanted me to source vintage-patterned hankies to do something similar for her wedding, which I did.

The dominoes continued to fall in my favor. The woman happened to be a well-known wedding photographer, and she shared the hankies on her own blog. Within hours, I had a rush of inquiries from customers all over the world. Soon after, *Martha Stewart Weddings* got in touch to say it was featuring me and the hankies on its website. I had stumbled into a niche world where people were looking for something different, something personal, for the most important event of their lives.

Doing the invitations made me feel something again, allowed me to create again, put me in touch with the part of me that had wanted to be an artist in the first place. It was liberating, a life raft to a drowning soul. I knew I was lucky, that opportunities like that come rarely, if ever.

Now I dived into my once spirit-crushing lunch break with renewed purpose. I would take my microwave dinner to my cubicle desk and work on teaching myself JavaScript or

My handkerchief invitations put my little freelance business on the map, though I never intended it to happen that way.

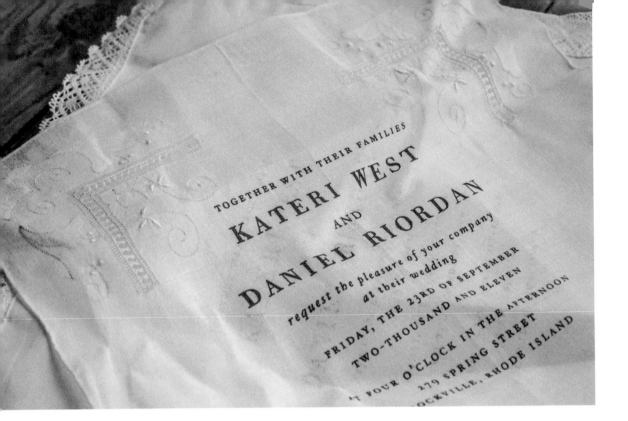

TOGETHER WITH THEIR FAMILIES

KATERI WEST

AND

DANIEL RIORDAN

request the pleasure of your company

at their wedding

FRIDAY, THE 23RD OF SEPTEMBER

TWO-THOUSAND AND ELEVEN

AT FOUR O'CLOCK IN THE AFTERNOON

279 SPRING STREET

ROCKVILLE, RHODE ISLAND

work on new designs. Lucky Luxe was open for business during my lunch break and from the moment I went home from work to the second I collapsed from exhaustion, usually around 1 a.m. The next step was to figure out a way to help people find me in the vast online ocean. Sam helped me build a website that would lure brides who were scrolling through countless other sites.

No matter how busy things got for me, I made a point of trying to understand exactly what was right for each customer. First, it required getting a sense of who the customers were. I would send a survey to the couple that dug deep into who they were and what they loved, their favorite books and music, and any details about their relationship or love story they wanted to share. The invitations would need to reflect the couple's life, love, and personalities.

Once I had that information as a jumping-off point, I would design three original concepts for the invitations. The couple would choose their favorite, which I would edit as needed and then build an entire paper suite around (the RSVP, directions, and so on). Once it was approved, I'd send it to my letterpress man, Friedrich, in New Orleans. Three weeks later, the invitations would arrive and I would ship them off. I loved the work and was honored to play a part in bringing weddings to life. Even with the late nights, tight deadlines, and in-over-my-head craziness of the venture, there was a magic to all of it.

Of course, I still had to show up at work every day and was dutifully in my cubicle by 8:05 a.m. But the sameness of a day job became maddening, especially when I had something so tempting

ABOVE: Shopping for vintage handkerchiefs became a part-time job for my part-time job. I was always most thrilled to find a lot of 100+ where fewer than one-quarter had holes or stains.

The decision came down to something simple: ignoring or listening to myself.

and freeing waiting for me outside those electric blue walls. My eyes were constantly on the clock, which became my jailer and my redeemer, locking me in from eight to five and giving me freedom in between.

Months passed, and I grew sick with boredom and consumed by stress. I was mad at myself for simply surviving, annoyed that I didn't have the courage to leave my job, exhausted from the lack of sleep. I tried to balance two lives, one that was my living, the other that felt as though it were keeping me alive.

I was pushed and pulled in two directions, faced with a clear choice: I could remain where I was, stable and protected and dying on the inside. Or I could trust in myself and take a leap of faith that frightened and excited me in all the right ways. I'd wake up in the dark of night, my clothes soaked in a cold sweat, hit with cresting waves of nausea. Then I'd just lie there as light crept through the windows.

The decision came down to something simple: ignoring or listening to myself.

I needed to get over my fear of going out on my own, to muster the courage to quit my job, but I would invariably talk myself out of it. I was my parents' child, pragmatic before anything, remembering that the one guarantee in life is that there are no guarantees.

It was a rough time physically, emotionally, and psychologically. Stress took on different forms

and attacked my body. I barely had time to neglect the laundry and the cooking. God love Ben, though, he took up my slack, always without complaint. When Lucky Luxe had gotten going, Ben and I had agreed on one thing: I wouldn't turn away any business. We pledged just to figure it out.

I gave it everything I had, and without Ben, it would've broken me. Ben made dinner, washed the clothes, and kept everything in order, including me. I would cry to him, and he would tell me to pray about it. Ben's confidence in me was liberating; he was sure it was time to take that step and go out on my own. I was lifted by that but uncertain, so I did what I usually do when faced with such a decision: I talked to my parents.

When he was young, Daddy had had the opportunity to start his own private practice, but my grandfather advised him to stick with the stability of his job at the hospital. Daddy had followed his advice and decided against opening the practice, but the ghost of that decision still haunts him, as he never stopped wondering what might have been. From then on, my dad was reticent about offering his children advice for fear of misguiding us. "Sugar, every bucket's got to sit on its own bottom," he said. "I know you and Ben will do the right thing. Pray about it."

And so we did.

The students of Laurel First United Methodist Church.
These folks gave Erin and me a lot of joy over the decade I was in youth ministry.

8

A Faith

Ben

Growing up, I loved my family, Duke basketball, and Jesus.

Faith was a permanent and unquestioned part of my life. My family—everyone around me, really—was cut from that same cloth. We were churchgoers and Methodists, and those facts permeated just about every aspect of our lives. It was an intimate part of me, as connected to me as an arm or a leg. It was the air from which I drew breath.

Faith is different for everyone, determined by the way each of us is wired. For me, my faith operates as both a floor to ground me and a ceiling to reach for. It champions me and humbles me. It connects me to the larger community, and it makes me feel singular. It tells me I'm one of many, while making me feel as though only I can stand on the spot where I'm standing. It questions me, and it guides me. It reminds me that no matter how good things get, we could lose everything tomorrow. And it assures me that no matter how bad things can be, it's all going to be okay.

I'm a preacher's son and people person, so working in youth ministry felt like the obvious path for me. It was something I fell into. While I was in high school, a counselor had spoken to me about working in youth ministry and I'd substituted for the youth director at our local church during my senior year. At Ole Miss I got a job as a youth director, which not only kept me afloat on the rent and bills but gave me another kind of family through the church. I spent my teenage years so involved in our churches, day in and day out. That's how it usually is for preachers' kids, but I loved everything about it: the boring breakfasts with the old men, the awkward sing-alongs, the heavy conversations about life and spirituality, sharing things there you would never share anywhere else. My goal as an adult working with teenagers was that they be able to connect with God the way I once had.

When I moved to Laurel after college, I got a job as youth director near Hattiesburg, about forty-five minutes away, where I worked while also taking a swing at that graduate degree.

I gave it the old college try, but graduate school was simply not for me. If I'm completely honest, I have to admit I hated every minute of it. Soon after starting classes, I recognized that my love of history didn't translate to the graduate level: I loved stories, heroic moments, and consequential events, unique characters and brilliant minds, the reckoning of two sides coming together or a crisis coming to a head. But graduate school for history is focused on theory, research, and methods. It's dry as a hay barn in August, and I was bored out of my mind.

Plus I was burned out. I had been going full steam for two years at Ole Miss to keep up with the workload and to graduate on time with Erin, carrying more than a full load each semester, taking intercession classes during each break and summer sessions just to reach the finish line on time. When I first hit the wall at graduate school, I figured I just needed a break and considered taking some time off to regroup. I was already working full-time as a youth director, renovating the loft, and getting involved with local Laurel community matters. But the very desire to take time off was a red flag; I eventually accepted that I wasn't cut out for graduate school, nor was it cut out for me. Once I'd decided that, it was like a weight mercifully lifted off of my shoulders. You can't force a thing like that, a lesson I'd learn and relearn more than once in my life.

Even though I had scrapped my master plan, I wasn't too worried. I'd already established myself

ABOVE: Some of our students at camp. They were a tight-knit group at Laurel FUMC.

TOP LEFT: Laurel FUMC at Lake Junaluska in 2013. | TOP RIGHT: Ricky, Shark, and Jonathan and a group hug. BOTTOM: Erin and me at camp in 2008.

Lake Junaluska

In the mountains of western North Carolina, there is a hamlet of early-1900s homes surrounding a lake in a valley of green mountains on all sides. The Methodist Church established it as a retreat for ministers, and it became the headquarters of the Methodist youth camps that I started attending in fifth grade.

At Lake Junaluska the air was always sweet and, even in summer, the swimming holes stayed ice cold. When I was a youth minister, I continued the tradition, taking students to Lake Junaluska, to hear their voices echo off the mountains when we would shout at the midnight service after walking to the cross. Some of my best childhood memories had happened there, and I wanted to continue that tradition for the kids in our church.

working with the United Methodist Church, a tight-knit community where word travels far and fast. About a year later, I was offered the full-time position at Laurel First United Methodist Church just one block from our loft, a church that already felt like home for us.

At the time I was in my twenties, not much older than the teenagers I was working with, not long removed from the worlds they lived in and the challenges they faced. There was an older-brother aspect to my work, which I loved; I could relate to them on their level, and they respected me enough to listen to me. Things clicked. I began to wonder if maybe it was my calling. It wasn't a realization like the one my dad had had on that tractor all those years ago; it just kind of gradually unfolded that way. I didn't have a reason to question it, so I didn't.

As I was finding my footing with my new students in Laurel, planning a year's worth of programming and leading discussions, I got into a natural groove. Most of my students had grown up in the church, much as I had. But I also had the opportunity to work with kids whose families weren't involved in church, who had not grown up with faith, who had parents who hadn't taken an interest in their spirituality. Some of my students had single moms who were working extra shifts on the weekends, so there wasn't much time for much else. Others came from families who attended church somewhere else but they had lost interest when they had become teenagers. It was fascinating seeing how much those kids in particular were drawn to our lessons. Because they hadn't grown up embedded in the church, they seemed more eager to find faith in something. It was as though they had discovered it on their own, and because it was powered by their own interest and curiosity, the attachment was more solid.

ABOVE: Me and my sister-in-law Lyn at Lake Junaluska in 1999 when I was in youth group.

These were impressive young people, coming to our meetings on their own accord, finding ways to get there without cars, looking for a place in which to explore their faith rather than the alternatives. They were genuinely interested in hearing what He was saying. My work brought with it a weight of responsibility, and I took it all seriously.

We would have long, heavy discussions about issues they were dealing with or were on the cusp of dealing with or were worried that they wouldn't have the capacity to deal with when the time came. It reminded me of the talks I'd once had with my mother, which had laid the foundation of who I was as an adult. It was an honor to play that role for those kids, who were beginning to take their faith—and their lives—seriously. At an age when distractions and temptations are everywhere, when it's very difficult to get kids to participate in anything faith based, those kids had both feet planted solidly on the ground. Months turned into years, and I watched them transform into young adults before my eyes. They would grow up and go away to college again and again, heading out into the world to become who they were going to be.

Each year I'd give the students my yearly "Come to Jesus" speech about the value of their uniqueness. "God made one of you," I told them. "There's only one. You've got to be who you really are, who He intended you to be, which is unlike anyone else, uniquely you, in your faith, your beliefs, your relationships, and your interests, to play your part in the body of the church and find meaning in your life."

Those were simple truths with enormous power. Believing them and living by them could change everything about their future. Following the blueprint God made for you doesn't mean you'll be perfect or holier than or a model example of faith, honesty, and greatness. It doesn't mean that you won't fail constantly, because you will. But if you do, you'll hear Him whispering, "It's okay. That's in the plan. Now, keep going and keep your eyes on me. I'll help you."

I also read them "The Message," from Romans 12:2: *Don't become so well adjusted to your culture that you fit into it without even thinking. Instead, fix your attention on God. You'll be changed from the inside out. Readily recognize what He wants from you, and quickly respond to it. Unlike the culture around you, always dragging you down to its level of immaturity, God brings the best out of you, develops well-formed maturity in you.*

> "God made one of you," I told them. "There's only one. You've got to be who you really are, who He intended you to be, which is unlike anyone else, uniquely you, in your faith, your beliefs, your relationships, and your interests, to play your part in the body of the church and find meaning in your life."

I tried to focus on giving them a general understanding of the Bible, something that could be a moral compass for them, and the three graces, which are part of Methodist theology.

Youth ministry was never really my goal in life; it was just something that came easy to me. I was outgoing, I had a strong faith, and I had a built-in support system through my parents and their friends, who were also ministers. If a student had a deep theological question, I didn't have to fake my way through it; I could go to someone higher up for more perspective. But one aspect that was difficult was dealing with parents—of all stripes. I had to learn quickly how to adjust my approach when talking with parents and keeping them abreast of their child's progress.

I never sought the job and I couldn't say that it was my passion, but it seemed to fit like comfortable clothes. At some point, that didn't seem like enough. Though I loved bonding with the kids, something about ministry as a job never seemed quite right for me. I never really asked myself if it was something I wanted to do. It's just what I did.

One spring night Erin and I were sitting on the stairs of our loft with the door open, the chirping of the crickets bouncing off the dark stairwell. She and I spoke constantly about the daily grind, the ups and downs of each day, but rarely would we discuss the big-picture status of our lives. We called those discussions our State of the Union talks, and they were as rare as they were significant. The talks consisted of things we both wanted to say but would put off because it was all too much to take in at once.

"Hey, Big," Erin said. "Talk to me. Work. The youth program. What's going to happen? I mean, in five years?"

Without meaning to, Erin had stepped on a land mine. Or rather, she had pushed me into one. It was the one question that I had been putting off answering, the one I could see out of the corner of my eye but wouldn't look at directly. I just couldn't picture myself becoming an elder in the church or the leader of a congregation. I had always believed that I would one day age out of youth ministry, but that day never seemed real until that night on the stairs when I was fumbling for an answer. It was as though I had been driving on a road with my headlights off and it didn't occur to me until Erin leaned over and flicked them on.

The confidence I've always had, the confidence that everything would always shore up, was being tested. That night, with Erin asking me about the future, it was as though God was speaking through her.

Another thing that seemed to set things off had to do with my youngest brother, Jesse, who was finishing his last year of high school. It's hard to explain, but my family is such an intimate part of my life that I tend to see most things through the lens of them: the ministry is wrapped up with my dad; how I treat Erin—and all women, really—is wrapped up with my mom; my friendships are all in some way variations on what I have with my brothers. So something about Jesse graduating felt like a crossroads, a moment to pause and take stock. He had been my inside man, giving me perspective on people his age, offering advice when I was hitting a block with a particular student.

Jesse was like the last line tethering me to the world of youth; it was being cut and soon I'd be floating on my own, getting older and becoming more distant from those I had promised to guide. Their

culture, interests, technologies, and social networks were becoming foreign, rapidly evolving in a way with which I couldn't keep up. As the new generation was coming up, the distance I felt from them was not just numerical but social and cultural.

I could've powered through the way I always had, but the fissures were starting to show. The job no longer felt like the right fit. Ministry is not the kind of thing you can fake or do halfway. I know that first and foremost from my dad; the ministry was his life, inside and out. Being a minis-

ter was who he was, on the most elemental level. When I looked at myself, surrounded by people certain that the ministry was their lives, I wasn't sure what I saw.

All of a sudden my future seemed cloudy. I found myself wondering about what was next, how much longer this could last, what the alternatives were going to look like. Quietly, my career, my plan, my foundation was cracking—and I couldn't ignore it. Until I did something about it, the cracks would only grow and spread.

ABOVE: Every year, leaving camp at Lake Junaluska, we would take a group photo at the cross.

For Christmas the year I left the cubicle, Ben gave me those metal letters to serve as my first "signage" in my studio.

9

A Purpose

Erin

When we are young, we take chances.

I am not, by nature, an optimistic person. I cling to hope and the kindness of others and the rightness in the way the world sometimes is. But I've always been afraid that if I don't manage my expectations, the other shoe will drop. Whether that other shoe is comeuppance, failure, or just the universe balancing itself out, I can feel it lurking. It might be just out of sight, but it's unmistakably there. My fear acts as armor; my feeling is that by preparing for the world to crumble, perhaps I can keep it from happening. If I assume everything is always going to be great, I'll jinx it. It's a superstitious sort of pessimism I have.

Ben and I have been blessed a million different ways and no tragedy has befallen us, so maybe there's something to this managing of expectations. It's a burden, though, one I've always hated carrying. It would never occur to Ben to think like this, of course, but for me it always felt like a way to stay protected.

For instance, when Ben and I met, he seemed genuinely interested in me, in the things I said and believed in and felt. He didn't just look at me, he saw me. He heard me. But my excitement was tempered by a dark thought, one I'm a little embarrassed to admit: I wondered if it was a prank. Like one in the corny teen movie where the popular guy dates the artsy girl on a bet. I couldn't accept that he was genuinely falling for me the same way I had for him. It just didn't seem possible. That's my brand of pessimism.

In the years since, Ben's warm and loving optimism has rubbed off on me. I am who I am, but spending my life with someone who has such positivity has opened me up to life's possibilities.

As much as I hate change and uncertainty and the damaging storms they can bring, I know that they are needed: they can unearth details in the house that is my life that may have gotten buried through disuse over time. Perhaps our real passions sometimes just need a little commotion to thrust them to the surface, then a dusting off to make them shine again. They might be buried or even forgotten. But once they come to light, we are so happy they're there.

It was an unsustainable path I was on. I was serving neither the company that had been so good to me nor the new opportunity that I had, in some sense, wandered into with Lucky Luxe. Both doors were impenetrable. I didn't know what was behind either one; I could only visualize, and I was hampered by the anxious monologue that was always running through my head. I could picture it: leaving a steady career with dreams of making it on my own and being humiliated, forced to carry a gigantic fool-headed mistake. Embarrassed that I had been exaggerating Lucky Luxe's potential, delusional that it could be a successful business. On my more hopeful days, I could see the other path, too: the freedom of scheduling my own day, working on something that gave me goose bumps, committing myself to something that would leave an impression in the world in some small way. I could see to a future where I'd be relieved that I had taken the leap.

I sought counsel from Ben, our friends, family, and the church, yet no one and nothing pulled one way or the other. Then, after months of praying and struggling with what to do, the answer came in such crystalline detail from the most un-

likely place. It changed my perspective and ultimately my life.

Hope, my best friend from high school, had been working as a missionary in the Philippines. Phone calls were too expensive, so our friendship relied heavily on broken-up Skype calls and emails. I'd told her I had started my own business on the side, but I'd never wanted to burden her with my First World problems, so I hadn't gone into much detail. She was doing important things with the International Justice Mission and working in an orphanage, so our conversations revolved mostly around her experiences.

One morning, though, she sent me an email, apropos of nothing.

Subject:
a little encouragement from manila

hey,
read this this morning. I think it will be good for you as you consider what to do about your job. I hope this helps in a small way!

Love you-
hope

Below was the text of a devotional from *Streams in the Desert: 366 Daily Devotional Readings* by L. B. Cowman[1]:

Wherever God's finger points, His hand will clear a way. Never say in your heart what you will or will not do but wait until God reveals His way to you. As long as that way is hidden, it is clear that there is no need of action and that He holds Himself

---

[1]L. B. Cowman, ed. James Reimann, *Streams in the Desert: 366 Daily Devotional Readings,* rev. ed. (New York: Zondervan, 1999).

accountable for all the results of keeping you exactly where you are. For God through ways we have not known will lead His own.

As I read, a feeling caught in my chest. I recognized it immediately, unmistakably. It was like an old friend. I genuinely believe we have to "mind the checks" from God, the cues and signs He sends. They might not be in a language we understand, and they usually come forth in a whisper, but we know them when they arrive. They come on unexpectedly and like a gentle urging. It's a sound, an energy that can be easily ignored but not forgotten.

Something about that email, with that quote from that person at that time, clicked everything into place. It was as though His finger had been pointing to my true path for many months and then His hand had cleared away the fog of doubt.

It was the perfect time, place, and season of my life to strike out on my own. I was a newlywed with creative energy to burn, the skill set, and just the right amount of nerve to do it.

I was afraid of what would come, but I trusted the half of my gene pool that is my daddy—the bullheadedness that made my parents nervous when I was a teenager and proud when I became a woman. I knew I would always work hard enough to keep my head above water. And I trusted the half of me that was my mama—the part that would allow me to stay open and tender enough to know when something wasn't working and change it.

If my passions hadn't shifted so abruptly to building a company of my own, I might have built my career from that cubicle. In hindsight, I know that the job itself was never miserable; it was just that my heart had been stolen by something else, something so compelling that was pulling me toward it. I was fortunate to have that job and salary, especially right out of college, and I'll always be grateful for the experience. I knew that quitting would be difficult; my bosses had reached

Ben

I never thought she would do it. Erin is practical by nature. She has a work ethic like her dad, who has done the same work at the hospital since 1975. She's very much his daughter. When she was on the fence about quitting, she talked to mentors and colleagues from the ad agency in Memphis. They all advised her to quit. "When you work for a company, you have one client. You lose that client, you lose everything. Work for yourself, and the whole world is your potential client," they told her. But she wouldn't listen. She had ministers telling her, "Listen to your heart and listen to your faith. You'll know the right thing to do." And she still wouldn't do it.

When I was a kid, my dad gave up everything we had to be a minister. So I didn't carry the same fear she had that quitting her job would be catastrophic. My dad did it and everything turned out okay. We still had food on the table, we still had each other, and Daddy was happier.

She didn't know if it was going to pay off, but she was rewarded in a massive way. In the beginning, it was like watching her in college again—she had rediscovered that passion. Every day was something new and incredible, and if you've ever been around a creative person, if they don't have that spark, they become a bit empty, like the light has shut off inside of them.

Self-employment might be tough, especially in the beginning, but she kept her eyes on the positive to guide her through. It was an incredible thing to witness.

out a hand to a young woman fresh out of college who needed it.

With that in mind, I hemmed and hawed about giving my two weeks' notice.

I would start the email to my boss, only to delete, then rework, then delete it again.

"While I am deeply grateful for the experience and the work I've done here, I have made the decision to pursue entrepreneurship . . ."

Backspace.

"Thank you for taking a chance on me as a newly minted graphic designer. I've enjoyed my time here . . ."

Delete draft.

Again.

Again.

I'll try again next week, I told myself. When the timing feels right.

* * *

My fear of the future, which would now rest on my own ability and determination, was paralyzing. But empowering, too.

I was scared. And I loved the feeling. I just could sense that it was where my best self lay: only commotion was going to unearth it. I would bring on the storm.

In December 2009, I wrote the final draft to my boss.

Rarely are we given moments when a single action will change everything—where one move is going to tip it all over. Movies make it look as though they happen to us every day, but we know they're rare. That's exactly why movies are made about them. I knew that I was in the midst of such a moment.

So I hit "Send."

> *It's all in our hands: what we choose to remember, pay attention to, look forward to.*

. . .

The first day of my self-employment, January 1, 2010, I woke up motivated with passion and purpose. That morning I felt like two wholly different people merging into one: equal parts fear and hope, small potatoes dreaming big, a kid doing my best impression of a professional. I had the fiery determination to make my business thrive and the desire to embrace every mundane task from the moment I woke up until the moment I went to sleep.

With anxiety always lurking just beneath the surface, I decided to follow Ben's lead. His anniversary books, which documented the highlights of the previous year, were an inspiration to me. They were not just gifts but acts of joyful creation, a packaging of our lives into a story we would tell and retell ourselves. "We can choose to be miserable or we can choose to be strong," the saying goes. "The effort involved is the same."[2] It's all in our hands: what we choose to remember, pay attention to, and look forward to.

I took Ben's anniversary books out of my nightstand.

As I read through them, my heart swelled at the memory of so much goodness and love. I realized that the only remedy I could find for my fear would be to erase my anxiety with blessings, written down, counted, and remembered. The thought inspired me to do something. To make something.

I vowed to consciously document the best thing that happened every day in an online journal, which I titled "Make Something Good Today." My hope was that writing it all down would shore up my resolve to make my business more than a dream.

And it worked. That year I focused on doing what gave me and the people around me joy. I cooked. I taught a painting class at the church. I joined a women's Bible study group. I traveled. I took time off when I needed it. I walked every morning. I spent time with my parents. I made things with my own two hands.

I changed my life and vowed to never forget that even on the worst day, there is at the very least one thing to be thankful for. Documenting held me accountable because I am stubborn and strong-willed, and I refuse to quit once I start something of my own accord. By creating it, I made sure it would always be there.

On the bad days—and there were plenty—I'd consciously try to search out the positive or make good things happen so I wouldn't be empty-handed at night when it came time to write a journal entry. I would be accountable to my own expectations and promises and made the conscious decision to forget the things that weighed on or nagged at me, to swim in the messiness of life, to be kind to people who weren't kind to me. The goal was to do, find, and be whatever it is that gives me joy rather than just wish for it.

Writing down only the good moments of each day was my way of controlling the narrative of

[2]Carlos Castaneda, *Journey to Ixtlan: The Lessons of Don Juan* (New York: Washington Square Press, Reissue Edition, 1991), 184.

TOP LEFT: In Full Bloom, a design inspired by garden weddings. | TOP RIGHT: Recognize that dress? *Photo by Brooke Davis*
BOTTOM LEFT: Blue, a summer suite inspired by Greece.
BOTTOM RIGHT: Market, my favorite design in my whole collection, inspired by French textiles.

our life. Even though I was out of control of the events of the day, writing what I chose to remember changed life as I knew it. A shift in perspective made a shift in me because the uncertainty of faith had always been so hard for me to grasp. This was a way to marry proof and faith; as time went on, the good things became more real to me than the bad. It was a callback to a song we had learned in the church nursery: "Count your blessings, name them one by one." It was a way to make my faith become more real than my fear.

The journal was an exercise in selective memory, of focusing on what matters in the time I have to spend on this earth, in this body. Most days were spent combating my genetic disposition for worry, but in between burned bright moments of a happy, satisfied life.

If I had never started the journal, I would have missed so much, taken the lessons for granted and without the gift of seeing the big picture.

I have always cherished stability. The decision to leave my day job, which for me meant leaving solid ground, was a gigantic leap of faith. But once my feet were in the air, my need for independence came rushing back to me. It emboldened a part of me that for years had taken the safe and cautious path.

That first winter, as I worked to find my footing, I knew I was onto something. I began to realize that I was living exactly, precisely the kind of life I had always wanted to live. Everything had changed, but it was not just the work or the location. It was me. It was how I had chosen to see my life.

I began to see just how many paths were open to me, some conventional, some not. So I set my sights on the life I was in the midst of building and envisioned the life I wanted so badly. And I knew that for my ambitious dream to be reality, I would need to go with the ebb and flow of it.

If ever I found myself sinking too far into luxury, the terrifying possibility of returning to the drudgery of the cubicle lit a fire under me. If ever I lost my gratitude in the middle of a stressful job, I would roll away from my desk and breathe, try to feel inspired by the beautiful old flatiron building we'd made into our home. I'd lean into the gratitude I felt for that perfectly unusual, creaky home we'd built. And, like magic, my stress would thin out into the air and a rush of creativity would take its place.

I would wake up, put on Django Reinhardt, and pretend I was the heroine of a Woody Allen movie, as if Paris and New York were just a red-eye away. To me, it was just as well that I was ten feet from my kitchen and a hundred feet from the door that led outside to a world I could enter anytime I felt the urge.

I loved our home, and it was a privilege to work there every day. I relished walking through the rooms each morning—turning the lamps on, starting the coffee for Ben, lighting an apple-scented candle in the kitchen. After breakfast, I would head to my office, where there stood a library card catalog made of oak, a gift from Dr. Wallace, a local pharmacist from our church, that I used to store invitation samples. I'd sit at my computer in my favorite soft, old button-down and the eyeglasses I had once worn only at bedtime and ease into my work like a warm bath, the very opposite of the way it used to begin, like being shoved into a cold shower. I usually began the day with correspondence. As word of Lucky Luxe spread, I'd answer interview questions for wedding blogs

TOP LEFT: Phone calls were rare; I mostly worked via email since my clients were on every continent. | TOP RIGHT: Woodland, inspired by bohemian woodsy weddings. | CENTER LEFT: A photo shoot for Lucky Luxe *Photo by Bethany Byrd* | CENTER RIGHT: I taught a painting class one spring! | BOTTOM LEFT: Carmela, inspired by an Italian wedding. | BOTTOM RIGHT: The Hemingway invitation, inspired by airmail from the early twentieth century, was one of the first Lucky Luxe designs.

and magazines and inquiry emails from potential clients from California to Australia.

The morning would be spent ironing vintage handkerchiefs for upcoming projects or packing and shipping the latest save-the-dates. My shipping desk had been built for me as a gift by Mr. Jack, an older, sturdy man with pork-chop sideburns, suspenders, and a rolled-up beanie like a lobsterman's. He had been hired to dismantle my great-grandmother's house, the same old Victorian that my aunt Mae had lived in when I was a child, and built the desk from the pieces. Ben had meticulously helped him by designing every storage cubby and shelf to make a space for cellophane wrap rolls and the spray paint cans that I used to edge-paint the cards.

We wanted to keep every chipping inch of paint that was clinging to each board so I could always remember the colorful interior of the farmhouse where I had watched *True Grit* and made scrapbooks of leaves. In the midst of working I could look at the desk and remember the gray porch floor where Aunt Mae had once rocked me on the chairs while waiting for my mama.

I remembered the teal-and-seafoam-green kitchen walls and cabinets, where the slanted old linoleum floors had felt like a fun house, the light yellow boards from her bedroom walls, the hinges of the cabinets from her screen doors that would creak and clap shut.

When almost all of the lumber was later lost in a fire, the desk was all that remained of my family's

ABOVE: The shipping desk made from what was left of Aunt Mae's house after it was demolished.

My Design Process

Each project had a different tone and energy, but the process remained the same. Whether invitations or homes, a version of this same process follows.

1. The fonts. *What fonts describe the very best version of this couple? What fonts express the mood of the event? The playfulness or elegance? The never ever ever Zapfino-ness?*

2. The ornamentation. *Antique florals? Spanish tile motifs? A tiny engraving of a horse from the nineteenth century? What would make the perfect visual to describe the event? How much ornamentation would be too much or not enough? Or would letting the invitation breathe without any ornamentation make the truest, purest statement?*

3. The materials. *Fabric or paper? Vellum or kraft? Extravagant or low-key? The material the invitation is made from communicates a cue for the guest to understand the formality or casualness of the event.*

4. The colors. *Deep navy cover stock with gold foil print or airy bright white watercolor paper with barely there dove gray letterpress ink? What would make the appropriate statement for these people, for this day?*

5. The alchemy of it all. *I would search for the common thread in these three things: the couple's love story, the things that matter to them about the wedding day, and the location of the event. Succeeding in finding that common thread and creating a visual package based upon it was a type of magic. And the couple could feel it right away.*

old homestead. Ben and Mr. Jack had turned the house of my memory into something right there in front of me. It would be a common theme in our lives: taking on something from the past, something maybe even forgotten, and breathing new life into it.

At lunch, Ben would come home from the church and we would walk to the coffee shop around the corner for sandwiches or soup, then take our afternoon stroll all over the historic district. We'd talk about our days or nothing at all, and I would breathe in the smell of the sweet olive growing around every corner. Afterward we'd each return to our work, and I'd head back home, starting a load of laundry or putting dinner into the slow cooker. Then back into the sun-soaked office with a peach Nehi in a glass bottle to begin designing that day's work orders.

Around 6 p.m., I would send off the proofs to my clients, then retire for the day. Ben would come home, and we might have a picnic supper on the rooftop or dinner in front of our giant windows, listening for the lonesome whistle of the train before it came thundering past and then the silence broken only by the chirping crickets. He would draw a bath for me piled high with bubbles, and after a long soak, we would watch a movie on the couch before bed.

I couldn't imagine anything that came closer to a perfect life for me. There was urgency and the desire to please, but I didn't feel pressured or stressed. I felt completely fulfilled.

In all the ways that mattered to me, I was home.

During those first sweet, perfect, self-employed days, we were always together,
and my gratitude was overwhelming.

I always loved her, but seeing her drive the Beetle, I was lovesick. Twitterpated. Infatuated.
I married the coolest girl on the planet.

10

Old Cars & Old Towns

Ben

*I'm a car guy, and as my friend Josh says, the right time to buy a classic car
is when your wife says she wants one.*

When Erin told me what she wanted, I thought it was sweet, exactly what I would expect from her. A car in the form of Erin, if that's possible. I asked her to make me a list of everything she needed in a classic Beetle, and I started looking for one that met the qualifications.

I was humoring her, to an extent. Her list was so specific that I knew it would be impossible to find: pearl white or candy apple red paint, tan or white top, tan tweed or light brown leather interior, good stereo with a CD player and iPod hookup, air-conditioning, and automatic transmission.

Sure thing. You got it, babe.

About a month later, a friend from church called to tell me that there was a convertible Beetle for sale on the edge of town.

As soon as Erin laid eyes on it, I knew we had just bought it. It was a 1971 pearl white Beetle convertible with a tan top and tweed interior, with just about every option she wanted. The one strike against it was that it was manual transmission, which Erin didn't know how to use. I promised that if she wanted the car, I would teach her how to drive it.

We settled on a price that included the trade-in of my first vehicle, a 1959 Studebaker Scotsman pickup. She cried and begged me not to trade in my truck, but I assured her that I didn't have time to get it restored anyway and that this was more important.

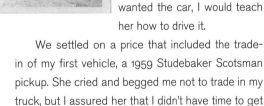

ABOVE: My old Studebaker that I traded toward Erin's Beetle.

That old truck turned up for sale a little while later, and though I considered buying it, I never regretted trading it in. Erin wanted that car far more than I would ever love that truck.

She named it Lucky.

The neighbors around Laurel High School came out of their houses to watch the spectacle of Erin learning to drive Lucky that night in the parking lot. The south entrance to the main parking lot was a short but steep incline. As we pulled in, she smoked the tires as though she were her older brother in his Mustang out on the back-road racetrack in Eatonville. She cried and gritted her teeth. She yelled at me that she wanted to go home. A man came walking up from a house on 10th Avenue in his wifebeater and gym shorts to give her pointers on getting her timing with her feet down.

An hour into it, she was ready to give up the car. I don't think I've ever laughed so hard in my life. I told her we weren't going home until she drove us there. I thought about my dad, who, when teaching me to drive a stick, had made me drive home from church. It had scared me, but it had given me the confidence to eventually drive on my own.

It was not too long after that she was burning up the roads all over town. I don't know who was more proud—her dad, her, or me.

That car looked good on her; it just fit her so perfectly. I would see her backing out of our driveway or downshifting coming to an intersection with her Ray-Bans on and a silk scarf tied in her hair, and my heart would ache for how much I loved this most unusual girl, different from anyone else I had ever met. Different in the best way possible. A comet in the night sky.

Erin

I'm sure Ben and I were born in the wrong era. We would have been right at home in the early 1970s, dating at the drive-in, listening to Motown, cruising to Phillips Drive-In for a #3 burger like our parents did in their shiny Chevrolets with the chrome door handles. I love, when I can, to extract the romance of the old days and bring it to the present. It's another form of choosing the life I want to live and the world I want to live in.

For me, it always comes back to the cars. Even as a young girl, I was enthralled by the magic of antique cars. Before I could even reach the pedals on one, I knew I loved them. That I wanted one. They were alive in a way that the other soulless plastic things on the road simply were not. In a flat world, they were three-dimensional, beaming with personality and history in a society preaching at the altar of the disposable.

When I was young, Drew Barrymore was the epitome of free-spirited, pixie-cut cool, and in the movie *Mad Love* she drove a yellow 1974 Volkswagen Super Beetle. She carried a kind of sex appeal born of her differentness. And that car and Drew's character merged in my imagination and stayed lodged in there.

When I turned sixteen, I begged my parents to let me have my grandfather's 1964 Pontiac, which had been passed down to Daddy. Because I am a bad driver with no mechanical skills, and because they love me, they said no. A 1995 Eclipse with a dent in the bumper was bought for me. Then my mom's Jeep was passed down; after I wrecked that, I got a 2000 VW Beetle that would happily suffice until the day I would buy my own antique beauty.

The day I bought Lucky, with the first money

TOP: I wanted to drive it so badly, but I didn't know how to yet.
BOTTOM: We swapped the ugly racing wheels that came on it for these originals by the end of the week.

The fact was, I couldn't experience the car the way he could. Lucky Bug was just a paper tiger if I couldn't drive her myself.

Years earlier, Daddy had tried to teach me on his manual transmission Jeep in my own high school's parking lot. It just hadn't taken. Though I understood the concept, my feet and hands couldn't find the rhythm, and the ordeal ended in frustrated tears. This time, as I turned the key with my left foot on the clutch and my right foot on the brake, I grimaced, waiting for the engine to buck and die, but was pleasantly surprised when I did the first step right. That was the only thing I did right for the hour that followed, which also ended in frustrated tears while Ben took my defeated, red face in his hands and kissed me square on the mouth, laughing at how worked up I was getting. "Try again, baby!"

A dozen infuriating tries later, I shifted from first gear to second and made a circle around the parking lot without event. My spirits were lifting as I kept going. I slowed down and parked, praying I could do it again with the same result. I put my foot on the clutch and shifted to reverse, and Ben asked me if I could drive over to the entrance on the hill. I slowly rambled over to that slight slope of asphalt that, for my crippling fear in the moment, might as well have been the incline of Lombard Street in San Francisco. He talked me through how it would work, and I clenched my jaw as my heart raced, ready to let go of the clutch and hit the gas at the critical moment to keep it from stalling.

I saw it in my mind's eye—puttering right through the traffic light on the hill by 16th Ave-

I'd ever made on my own, Ben drove us to Hattiesburg. The car had soul, and so did our soundtrack. With Elvis and Janis on the radio, we didn't care that the speakers sounded a little blown; we would replace them anyway. We screamed about how freedom's just another word for nothing left to lose, with that false sense of invincibility you get inside the wind tunnel of a topless convertible on the interstate. I felt jealous as I watched his big hands wrapped around the glossy black steering wheel, envious at how he shifted effortlessly. I could only imagine the power I would feel in being able to operate it.

nue. I wasn't afraid at all! I was an independent woman! I could drive anything!

And it stalled.

And I hollered and cried.

And I tried again.

Again.

Again.

Independence was mine, and it wasn't about my new career or my new car. It was about DOING instead of dreaming.

* * *

Independence was mine, and it wasn't about my new career or my new car. It was about doing instead of dreaming.

From the release I had felt when I hit "Send" on my two weeks' notice to the day I left the parking lot bent on conquering the busiest intersection in town, as long as I had rock-steady Ben in the passenger seat calming me down and building me back up, there was nothing but my own fear stopping me from going anywhere I wanted to go.

I would run my errands with the top down, the wind in my hair, the Drifters on the radio. I couldn't wait to feel the sun on my skin as I eased on down the road, grateful that some cars are made of steel and carbureted engines and you can drive a time machine such as this and be part of a time and place you've been homesick for even though you've never been there.

SUMMER 2010

There's something about the history and majesty of old towns. They tell us who we were, which helps us understand who we are. There's a tendency for us to forget or disregard the old in favor of the new, but Ben and I have always embraced it. Just as people come from somewhere, places and objects do, too; it's up to people to make sure they don't get buried and forgotten. This has been something of a mission in our lives.

That summer found us hitting the road on a leisurely five-hour drive with our bikes on the back and a cooler full of drinks. We swerved down back roads and through tiny towns across Mississippi, Alabama, and finally Florida, and made it to Wakulla Springs.

TOP: The high dive into Wakulla Springs will never not scare Ben, and he'll never not do it.
BOTTOM LEFT: The Lodge at Wakulla Springs is like visiting another era entirely.
BOTTOM RIGHT: We catch up on our reading at Wakulla without Internet or TV to distract us.

My aunt Cheryl, who is not actually my aunt, had been visiting there every summer for years. She and my mom have been close friends forever, and she had convinced us that we had to stay for at least one night on our way down to St. Augustine. Ben was elated: no Internet, no TV, no phone service. I'm another story, but Ben is built to unplug.

What would prove to be both the best and the worst part about owning my own business was that it was 100 percent up to me to run it. I marveled at the autonomy, but the reality meant that there were no true vacations. Ben knew me too well; he was under no illusion that I would leave work behind on our trip. It was just another suitcase we carried along with us. As long as we had a computer and a Wi-Fi connection, we could run Lucky Luxe from pretty much anywhere. Our pressmen handled all of the printing, and as long as we scheduled our shipping and handling days along with Ben's days off from church, we could go anywhere we wanted. We had been to the beach with Ben's brother and his wife and were planning a trip to New York City for the fall.

In Wakulla Springs we stayed at a very old, idyllic Mediterranean-style lodge hidden deep within the swamps of a national forest. It rose like an apparition from the earth at the end of a long, winding driveway covered by oaks dripping with Spanish moss that blotted out the sun. The lodge sat beside the deepest freshwater spring in the world, where manatees and alligators played next to a rope meant to keep swimmers in and creatures out. *Creature from the Black Lagoon* was filmed there, and entire mammoth skeletons had been pulled from the springs—two facts that give me shivers. The movie played on a quiet loop in the nearly silent

lobby, a grand and cavernous place, all marble with hand-painted motifs on the coffered ceilings. An enormous wood-burning fireplace sat empty, but its smell was everywhere, reminding me of Christmas out of context, a feeling I always liked.

The lodge wasn't tied just to America's past but to my own. My grandmother's family used to come to the very same place on vacation when she was a teenage girl. One night I had been at Mammaw's house in search of old family photographs for a gallery wall. When I opened the hope chest at the foot of her bed, I found a photo she had taken

of her sisters posing in front of the fanciest hotel they'd ever been to in their young lives. I took that photo along to Wakulla Springs and held it up to the hotel's current incarnation.

ABOVE: The photo taken by my grandmother of her sisters at Wakulla Springs. Or at least, I think it's her sisters! It's hard to tell.

The Atlas

We've got this old atlas we bought at a gas station in college that's tucked behind the driver's seat of our truck. It's ratty and outdated, but we keep using it. Ben has always believed in the paper atlas above the GPS because there's something great about finding our own way instead of

letting a computer algorithm determine our path. So he drives and I choose the route along with any diversions on the way. This method of travel has taken us everywhere from Micanopy, Florida, to Manchester, Vermont. We have found that there is no better way to see America.

The brass accordion doors of the elevator sprang shut to carry us to the second floor. In our room, I found a guest book with notes from previous visitors. Some claimed that a ghost had kept them awake at night; others said that they had luxuriated in a room that reminded them of the good old days.

The floors and walls of the bathroom were top-to-bottom mauve-and-tan marble that felt refreshingly cold on my hot summer feet. The room smelled clean and wet because the air-conditioning system used water from deep within the springs. Our windows cranked out over the clay tile roof, and I could hear the whippoorwills and frogs creaking together all around the springs that glow electric, the color of jade. There was no television or Internet, only the sounds of the mysterious woods and the faraway splashes and squeals of children making the brave leap from the high dive. Most of them were day swimmers, families who lived in the rural community for whom this was old hat.

I let myself unplug for the day, wanting to enter the place in mind and spirit as well as body. I wanted to see it the way Mammaw had as a teenage girl, ordering a Ginger Yip from the marble ice cream counter before wading cautiously into the freezing springs with an eye on the alligators just beyond.

The next day we drove across Florida to St. Augustine, my favorite place in the world. The place where my life had almost happened.

I've been visiting St. Augustine since I was ten years old, a tomboy in Umbros and a baseball cap with a ponytail through the back. Even then I knew that the oldest city in the United States was different from any place I would ever visit again. It was singular in a way that even a young mind can grasp. It wasn't an airbrushed tourist town or a manufactured stew of nostalgia; it was something altogether different. I could feel it in the air, and in my bones. I still can.

The Spanish moss on this old Florida two-lane highway casts a spell over me every time.

Mama used to tell me stories of visiting St. Augustine when she was a child on their way to Cape Canaveral. She was captivated by Ripley's Believe It or Not, a novelty museum of creepy wonders from around the world, which was housed in an old castle. My grandfather, a hardened World War II vet, kept a trolley ticket stub from that trip in 1967, a yellowed, ragged piece of paper that was more valuable to me than gold.

As Ben and I crossed rural marshes and bridges, I felt as though we'd driven into a seaside European town. Then the modern buildings on the outskirts gave way to ancient, authentic Spanish architecture near the heart of the city. Around every corner hid a new discovery, a little adventure: a secondhand bookstore, a lanky, leaning bed-and-breakfast with lanterns glowing on the porch, a vintage jewelry shop, an English restaurant with fish and chips, a city gate that's been standing rock solid since the early 1700s. I felt the breeze off Matanzas Bay, and I wanted out of the car so I could submerge myself in all of it.

Later we passed the sights that called up my childhood in bright color: the Butterfield Garage Art Gallery in an old service station; Villa Zorayda Museum, where I had once seen a mummy hand

TOP LEFT: Riding bikes to breakfast. | **TOP RIGHT:** Chapel of Our Lady of La Leche, a magical place of prayer.
BOTTOM LEFT: The Bridge of Lions. | **BOTTOM RIGHT:** Walking through the Plaza de la Constitución.

TOP LEFT: Our favorite restaurant, Columbia, at the intersection of St. George and Hypolita. | TOP RIGHT: St. Augustine Beach. | BOTTOM LEFT: Strawberry basil Popsicles: the way summer in St. Augustine tastes. | BOTTOM RIGHT: The French bakery closed a couple years ago after a century in business. We bought lots of croissants for our freezer so we wouldn't have to say good-bye and ate them as recently as last year, freezerburned though they were.

inside a glass case; cobblestoned Aviles Street with all different national flags hanging from the balconies; DeNoël French Pastry Shop, where the same family had been making the same croissants for fifty years; the grand Casa Monica Hotel across from Flagler College, the school that hadn't let me in, that couldn't find a place for me. The decision—someone else's—that had set me on the course I was still on.

Coming back again to that city, I realized that I didn't have to go there for it to become part of me. As I tried to do in my work and my journal and my life, I could just extract the good. I took away all the parts of that city that most affected me—the architecture, the history, the tall tales and hidden secrets—to call on when I need inspiration. Ben has to remind me often, "Everything'll turn out fine. It always has. Always will." He was right, as he so often is. Circumstance and luck have led to the only life that makes sense for me. There's an inevitability to it that brings me warmth, and I try to hold tight to that fact. I am where I should be. We are all where we should be.

ABOVE: Flagler College. The one that got away.

Baker and Clint in the garage.

11

A Forever Home

(Part I)

Ben

When you buy an old house, you have to earn the right to call it your own.

The people who once lived there are part of its story, and you can't just erase them—even if you want to. The foundation of that home isn't the concrete it's built on; it's the souls and the stories and the love embedded there. That's what makes houses so alive.

In Laurel, we refer to houses by the people who built them or whom the community remembers living there the longest: the Gilchrist House, the Hynson House, the Rogers-Green House. Erin and I have always been partial to the story and romance of old homes, so it was only a matter of time before we eventually found our own.

In the summer of 2011, during one of our walks through the historic district, Erin and I passed one of her favorite houses in Laurel. It was a modest yellow Craftsman cottage on a tucked-away street that she had been enamored with since she was a little girl. She used to drive through town with her mom

and look in awe at the beautiful homes that had been built long before her parents were born. Even through young eyes, she knew they held more secrets and beauty than the postwar ranch-style ones dotting the country roads where she lived.

She had gone through phases when she would photograph her favorite houses, including this one, and draw sketches from the pictures. During walks in college, we would pause in front of that cottage and I would watch Erin, as she was clearly seeing more than just the house in front of her. Her big imagination took hold like a storm.

One afternoon during our walk, we paused in front of it again. I recognized that look in Erin's eyes as she gazed at the cottage. "It's like a shy girl at a dance," she said, almost to no one in particular. "She's hiding off to the side, not knowing how beautiful she is."

As we stood there, an older woman came out onto the porch, with a broom in her hand. Both of us were surprised to see that it was Mrs. Mary Lynn.

Mrs. Mary Lynn was a recent widow and a beloved member of our church who makes a point of hugging every single person on Sunday mornings. She reminds me of late-era Jessica Tandy, a tiny woman with white hair, always impeccably dressed with tasteful jewelry, hair and makeup done perfectly. A genteel woman, she is classy and spry and full of joy.

"Hey, Mrs. Mary Lynn!" I said from the sidewalk. She looked up and waved. "We didn't know you lived here."

"This has been my favorite house since I was little!" Erin called out.

Mrs. Mary Lynn flashed a smile. "Really?"

"Yes!" Erin said.

"Well, y'all want to come inside?" Mrs. Mary Lynn asked. "I can show you around!"

Before I had a chance to politely decline, Erin jumped in. "We would love that!" she said, already

halfway up the front walk. I obliged; we're nosy if nothing else.

We went through the sage green foyer, stepping onto the polished heart-pine floors, passing manicured houseplants on stands. To the left was the formal living room, the walls painted lemon meringue. Sheer white drapes let the sun flood the room, dappling light on the wooden-armed sofas and polished mahogany end tables. I looked around the room and suspected that once-stained Craftsman trim work had been covered with white paint.

Mrs. Mary Lynn walked us through every room, each more polished than the last, talking about the house's history, how it had been built in 1925 for Laurel's first dentist, how she had lived there for little more than a decade. The French doors to the dining room were open, making the room feel enormous. The picture rails were unused, and the ceilings were high enough for a basketball hoop because back in the day before air-conditioning, that was the best way to invite a cool breeze in.

Then we stepped into her tidy light blue kitchen, which was disorienting, like stepping into a different time. Its Formica countertops and prefabricated

LEFT: The entryway, before we bought the house. | TOP: The living room, where we would add bookcases.

white cabinetry felt out of place, contradicting the rest of the impeccably designed home.

"If I had my druthers," Mrs. Mary Lynn said, "I'd change this kitchen. It needs help."

"Oh, yeah?" I said, feigning innocence.

"You bet," Mrs. Mary Lynn said, before launching into the story of how a hundred-year-old pecan tree had claimed most of the house in Hurricane Katrina six years earlier. The majority of the house had been restored after the storm, but "that tree steered clear of the kitchen, so . . ." She let the words hang there.

We all nodded, and I watched Erin. The wheels in her head were turning, as were mine. I was thinking of what could be done in that kitchen, the cabinets I could build, the butcher-block countertops I

could install. Woodwork was still just a hobby, but anytime I was in a home, my mind would start to imagine what could be done to it.

Mrs. Mary Lynn told us that in the 1920s, when Lauren Rogers, one of Laurel's founders' sons, had died suddenly at age twenty-three, his new home was still being built. His young widow had been so heartbroken that she didn't want to finish the house and live in it—nor did she want anyone else to. She had ordered it to be taken apart, and the salvage from the home had been used to build other houses all over Laurel, including this one, or so rumor had it. (Where the unfinished house once stood, the first art museum in Mississippi, the Lauren Rogers Museum of Art, now sits.)

As we left the house to continue our walk that afternoon, Erin casually blurted out over her shoulder, "If you ever decide to sell, just call us!"

Three days later, the phone rang. It was Mrs. Mary Lynn's daughter, Jennifer, who worked with me at the church.

"Mama is ready for the condo life," she told us. She was looking for an easier place with less

ABOVE: The kitchen before. The dollhouse trim was the first to go.

space and no yard to care for. "She thinks it's time for a young family to move in." I was struck by the generosity of spirit in her mother's reasoning, her big-picture view: She loved that place, where she and her husband had lived their story, so much that she wanted to pass it on to others who could start living theirs.

Years earlier, when we had finished renovating our loft, we'd thought we could live there forever. I'd even idly wondered how we could add an elevator for when we were too old to climb those stairs. But the fact was that by 2011, we had already outgrown that home. We still loved it, but it no longer fit the life we were living.

Erin's business had continued to expand, creeping into each room, literally pushing everything else into a corner. What had once been my office had been taken over by Lucky Luxe, the hallway and guest room had become sample storage, the odd room on the end was for shipping and handling, and our kitchen had become the product photography studio.

We loved that loft, its drafty windows and creaky wide-plank floors, and had settled into it like a comfy chair. It was our first home. It carried a romance and a connection to our story that we didn't want to let go of. We couldn't imagine finding—or even wanting—anything better.

But we knew that if we didn't buy Mrs. Mary Lynn's cottage, we might never have the chance again; we'd heard that lots of folks wanted to lay claim to it. I consider myself an amenable person, able to roll with—or dodge—the punches. I know that things don't arrive and depart exactly when you want, so you have to jump on the train when it shows up. Erin and I spoke about it a lot; she said

the thought of leaving the loft was heartbreaking, but the thought of someone else buying her dream home was worse.

> Whenever there is a lull or even a relaxing plateau, Erin gets a little antsy, maybe even lost.

She's never truly comfortable, but she's oddly the most uncomfortable when life seems easiest. She responds to action, the opportunity to make a situation better. So taking on a new home and the renovation work that came with it was exactly the kind of rising tide that lifted her up.

But she's also a realist. She was afraid that it was too risky, that we would be biting off more than we could chew, that we were doomed to sink in the flood of our own outsized dreams. But I knew we'd tread water. Then we'd swim. Then, one day soon, we'd flip on our backs and float comfortably.

I was up for the challenge and the journey for a project that size. I thought it would feed my soul. Work at the ministry had been imperceptibly fading as a future; somewhere in my mind, maybe I was looking for something big enough to excite, frighten, and bring out the best in me. And I had faith in Erin's verve, her resourcefulness, and her spirit; I knew that what she had built would continue to grow, that it would more than be able to fill our dreams.

So we kept the loft for her business, and bought the house that fall, loving it for what it was and for what it could be. We saw the house's beauty and its

possibility, embraced its past and its future, and had a vision of how it would fit into our story.

But it would take some serious work.

That fall and winter, renovation became our life. We were at the house every evening after work and every weekend, working side by side. At the end of each day, exhausted, we would drag ourselves to some fast-food joint at 10 p.m. to eat a burger before heading back to finish one last thing. I amassed more tools—table saws, miter saws, air compressors, nail guns—than I needed; it wasn't conscious, but in hindsight, maybe I was laying the groundwork for a future career, one that I hadn't considered yet.

As I learned how to run new electrical wiring, I also learned how not to do some other things, namely plumbing and sheetrocking. For those projects, I brought in a contractor. To this day, I believe in the importance of bringing in experts for projects that are not my forte. There's confidence and there's bullheadedness, and you just have to be realistic about where the line between them sits.

Our approach in renovating the home was simple: Hold on to the good. As Erin had with her journal, as we had with our lives, and as we would one day do for other people, we would hold on to the good and build everything else around that essential core. Our new house felt a lot like us when we bought it, so it was important that we didn't change its essential personality. We would simply adapt it to suit the kind of people we were.

For instance, the living room was more formal than we were, the kind of setup where the original owner's daughter had been married in front of the fireplace. Erin and I saw the room as the heart of the house, and we wanted it to have a more leisurely, homey feel. We added bookcases to hold our library of southern noir, American history, and woodworking. On a cold, rainy day, we wanted to be able to be worthless in front of the fire on a cushy sofa with a couple of books.

ABOVE: Building new cabinetry for the refrigerator enclosure.

TOP LEFT: Adding panel molding to the stairs below the handrail, before we removed the wallpaper and carpet and refinished the stairs. | TOP RIGHT: Plumbing the kitchen sink. | BOTTOM LEFT: Building new shelving for Erin's dream pantry. BOTTOM RIGHT: Custom built-ins I made to keep the dogs' stuff.

With a proper dining room, we would need a proper dinner table, so I set to work building one in my in-laws' garage. Eight feet long, made from the old columns of their front porch and the old floor of their back porch, the table would be another bridge connecting our past and future.

Erin wanted a deck at our back door, along with a bench and storage across from it for removing and collecting my muddy boots. We had a great love for built-ins and their perfect use of space. I had some really nice cabinet doors left over after a last-minute change to the kitchen layout, and I used oak stair treads for the tops of the built-in benches. My aim was for them to feel as though they were original to the house, as if a carpenter had built them back in 1925. Though I was a novice at cabinetry, the little gap around the doors was almost perfectly even all the way around, maybe just a little bigger than it should have been.

"Baby!" Erin squealed when she first saw them. "I can't believe you built this!" It's the single greatest exclamation a husband can hear. Sometimes I try to pull things off just to get the rush of hearing Erin say something like that. (If I'm honest, to this day, all I'm ever really trying to do is impress Erin.)

One by one, each room got a fresh coat of paint. Nothing against Mrs. Mary Lynn's colors—they were beautiful—but they weren't the colors Erin had dreamed about and scrapbooked for nearly twenty years. I'm not exaggerating. Erin had an accordion folder of magazine clippings that she had been collecting since the seventh grade. One thing I noticed while flipping through was that her personal style had changed very little in the last twenty years. She had torn the pages from her mama's *Southern Living* and *Coastal Living* magazines to save the worn wood furnishings, the white denim sofas, and the collected oddities used as artwork. The pass-through rooms of our new home got dark walls, and the main rooms were covered in Dover white, just as the scrapbook had foretold.

We'd put on Ray LaMontagne, order cheap pizza, and have painting parties with friends, replacing light fixtures, pulling up carpet, and hanging curtains.

We brought in our modest antique guest room furniture and lined what would be my closet with cedar; we renovated the stairwell, and I added simple millwork below the handrail. With every hour we spent at the new house, it began to feel more and more like ours. It was so tempting to move in right away, but after my experience renovating and living in the loft, we agreed that until we could walk through without stepping on a nail, we wouldn't. So we soaked in "firsts" before we had even spent a night under our new roof. We decorated our first front stoop with pumpkins, sat on our swing bench on our first porch, and handed out candy to our first trick-or-treaters, knowing all the while that we would one day bring our newborn babies home here.

As we had suspected from that first walk-through with Mrs. Mary Lynn, the kitchen was like the white whale. We planned to change the countertops, swap the places of the stove and fridge, and update the cabinet doors. But I wanted to take it a little further. After all, we were dealing with sacred ground: this would be the kitchen where Erin would teach our children how to make Mammaw's biscuits.

One day, on something of a whim, I went for the big swing. Literally. I decided to knock out the cute dollhousey boxes that were shading the tops of the windows. That one hammer swing created a domino effect that would lead to a complete gutting of the kitchen. When I knocked out the piece of decorative fascia to let in some more light, I also knocked out a

myself and it would eventually become my trademark. On a trip across Massachusetts through the small towns and into Boston, we collected a mix of cup pulls and hardware from schools and pharmacies for the kitchen cabinetry, a touch that would remind us of our adventures even when we were staying in place.

With newfound confidence, I moved on to overhauling the pantry. It was huge compared to the kind found in most older homes, but its pine board shelves, mounted on flimsy brackets, were awkward and oversized. Granted, nobody comes to your house and says, "I'd love to see your pantry!" but Erin felt it was a poor use of space and ugly to boot. I used the wood from the old shelves for most of the construction and bought a couple of other pieces to finish it out. It was my first experience with a wall that was not exactly square and plumb, something I didn't realize until after I had cut everything and was nearly finished installing. I powered through, and despite a few awkward lines, it turned out okay. Visitors never ask to see it, but if they did, I'd be happy to show them.

piece of it above the cabinets. One thing led to the next, and before I knew it, I had taken out the soffit, damaging the tops of the cabinets and tearing some of the old wallpaper that was mummified under the paint.

It was like drilling to the center of the earth. The farther I went, the more I discovered. All of that demo revealed some sheetrock work that would need to be done, so we decided to add new lights and scrape the popcorn ceilings. Since my demo had damaged the cabinets, we added crown to the tops. Then we found slabs of maple butcher block on the cheap and installed them ourselves as countertops, though soon after I was able to make those slabs

There were plenty of days when we felt as though we were spreading ourselves too thin: working, getting sick, hitting construction setbacks, and having day-to-day headaches like everyone deals with. But there was something else, something bigger that began to gnaw at Erin.

"It feels like everyone is having a baby but us," she said that fall. And that winter. And that spring.

ABOVE: We built a new garage in the backyard where I could work on cars and spent one afternoon together landscaping it.

And she was right—it did feel that way. Every time we'd hear someone's news, we'd feel a flood of joy for our friends or family, followed by a wave of sadness. Erin's heart would break just a little more, each phone call or announcement making a fresh new crack.

Growing up as a middle child, I'm the classic pleaser, always needing to fix whatever is broken. It's just my view of the world: something is broken, you give a hand and try to fix it. But it took me a long time to figure out something so simple: sometimes people don't want you to fix anything. They just want you to be there.

So Erin would cry, and I would hold her and let her cry. There was nothing else I could say or do to make it better. She needed to cry, and I needed to listen. It's not the easiest thing for me to do, even now, but it's what works. Sometimes love and support don't come from what you do; they come from what you are.

Her fears always circled back to what would happen with her business or what if we weren't even able to have children? Never mind the fact that childbirth had been her greatest fear since she was young and had first seen childbirth pictures in one of her dad's medical books; they were permanently tattooed in her brain. She was plagued by what-ifs, worst-case scenarios that seemed to chase her like ghosts. I never felt pressure to begin a family, figuring it would happen when God ordained that it was time. When Erin was ready to take that step, I would go with her.

"If you want to finish a project," my friend Josh taught me, "plan an event." Those are wise words; it's a chips-down kind of thing to do, and it has become somewhat of a mission statement for us. Whether it's a lighting project in downtown Laurel or a guest house renovation, this trick never fails. It loops in other people and plays on your desire to never let people down.

So we planned to host Easter weekend in a house that wasn't finished. It would be a good way of introducing everyone—Napiers, Rasberrys, and framily members—to our new home. We would figure it all out—light fixtures, missed patches needing paint, furniture—by the time Easter came around because we would have no other choice.

So much happened during the renovation that would lead us to the unlikely place we've found ourselves in today. For the first time, we were each using our specific gifts—Erin's knack for design and art and my passion for construction and history—to design a home around the owners: us. Uniting all those things would become our philosophy and our way.

This is what I know: the little updates and repairs you make yourself—even if they aren't perfect—are the things you'll be most proud of. There are things you need to call in the pros for, but anytime you can do something yourself, there's a kind of satisfaction there that is invaluable.

In building pieces for our house, I learned that I could retreat into my creativity. My brain could shut out everything else and focus on the world six inches in front of me. It was a blocking out, a kind of tunneling, that I would grow to crave. There's nothing that's better for a cluttered head than loud saws and splintered hands. The roughness and the noise transform into a kind of peace and quiet, an oasis, and I would find myself looking more and more often to seek it out.

We live on the front porch when the weather cooperates.

12

A Forever Home

(Part II)

Erin

There comes a point when you wake up and finally know that it's time to grow.

You find you have just an ounce more courage than you did the day before, and it makes all the difference. You take it as a sign or a nudge from God. You make a decision that changes your life.

In my work, I always begin with people. I see the people first and then try to design the world around them, one that speaks to them. It is a type of communing that is hard to find and impossible to fake. In the spring of 2012, by digging in together with our peculiar skills, Ben and I were ready to move into the house that I had loved and dreamed of and sketched on paper and in my mind for years.

At first it was hard for me to think of that yellow cottage as my own. But bit by bit through the time we spent working on it, we began to see our own personalities in those rooms. It would take more time, and some living in it, until it felt fully ours. Its history stretched so far back, past Mary Lynn and her husband and Laurel's first dentist, Dr. Haynes, and Lauren Rogers

and his heartbroken wife—back into a world we couldn't know.

Ben is right: a home just doesn't become yours because you bought it or because you moved in. There's another level at work, and it takes time and memories and love and experience to get there.

Home grounds us in both mental and physical ways. We long for it when we're away or when we are unsettled in the world, because it's a place that evokes a feeling of permanence. At Mama's house, there is always a cozy glowing light in every room, lamplight in every corner, the smell of baking apple crisp and fresh laundry, beds all white with fluffy down comforters.

Since Mama stepped into my grandmother's shoes as family cook there have always been hearty leftovers in the fridge: a salad with onions and tomatoes from their garden, catfish caught in their lake, a pear cake made with fruit from the backyard smothered in homemade caramel icing. That yellow kitchen, even when magazines and bills are spilling out onto the counters and she calls it a mess, is still one of my favorite places in the world. Kitchens carry the residue of history: families congregate in that space, events are prepared, stories are shared, and things are made.

I've since learned that you can have many homes if the magic of ordinary moments lives there. Until I lived with Ben, Mama and Daddy's house was my home; no matter where I lived, it's where my heart always was. Then my home became wherever Ben and my pajamas and books and photos were. For years that had been the second-story loft in the old building in downtown Laurel.

We could move our furniture and boxes and clothes and books to the new house, but that feeling wouldn't just move with them. It would take time for that feeling to transfer to our new home, for its Ben and Erin–ness to seep in and settle.

Change is a frightening thing. I was going to miss so much about being perched in our nest above the park: the feeling of going barefoot on our very creaky, uneven floors, the windows that were so easy to throw open, the way the train would plow past and shake plaster dust from the old walls, the sanctuary of our dark and quiet bedroom.

I had told Ben that I didn't want to tempt sadness by talking about it or saying good-bye. I just wanted to go to bed in the loft as if I would always go to bed there. "And tomorrow, we'll just go to bed somewhere else," I said. But sleep wouldn't come. Exhausted, Ben snored quietly next to me, but I was wide awake.

My brain had come to terms with the move, but my heart didn't feel quite ready to leave. It wasn't an entirely rational thing, but often the things that keep us awake aren't. I knew the move was the change I needed: it was a clear delineation of our next phase and would separate my work and home lives in a way that was healthy, but still . . . if you love something enough, it never feels like the right time to leave.

The next morning Mama was up with the sun and at the door of our new house in her running shoes and holding her vacuum cleaner, ready to help us organize every closet and stock every drawer. The fridge and pantry were full, the flower beds were mulched, the porch was washed. That coming weekend we would be hosting our families for Easter.

That first night in our new home, I couldn't help focusing on the differences between the two places, the way you might pick apart everything a new person does after a recent breakup. I noticed the way the wind did not get past the windows, which had been painted shut for decades. The train, once a rumbling thunderclap, was now just a lonely howl in the distance. When I got up in the middle of the night, I groped along the walls, searching for the bathroom in the dark, my feet padding across its waxed heart-pine floors, smooth as glass and silent.

Saturday morning, the day before Easter, Ben and I had breakfast in flannel pajamas in Adirondack chairs on the porch. As the sunshine was burning off the fog, we listened to birds chirping, the lilt of sprinklers, the sound of mailboxes squeaking open. It was particularly beautiful outside—neither hot nor cold, chilly enough to have a fire but warm enough to open the French doors.

It still felt as though we were visitors or on vacation somewhere, in a rented house in Savannah or St. Augustine. It wouldn't feel quite like our home until we had a chance to make memories in there.

Since Ben's family lived hours away and a preacher's family needs to be at church Easter morning, we had long planned to have them over that Saturday to introduce them to our new home. After a low-key Napier Easter cookout—grilled chicken, sausage, roasted vegetables, and macaroni and cheese—we all took a long walk around the neighborhood. Then Ben and his brothers threw the football in the front yard, while I went into the house with Ben's mother and sisters-in-law and set up an ice cream sundae bar on the front porch.

The next day, Lord help us, we hosted my entire extended family for Easter Sunday lunch. After church, we rushed home to beat my family there, but since everyone had brought their famous side dishes to go with the ham and coconut cake, I didn't have to do much more than point out where the drinks and plates were and answer questions about the house.

We somehow managed to cram around every table and chair we could scrape up. Daddy and Uncle Danny regaled us with stories of high school football and Conway Twitty concerts, and then my cousin Kent made us all howl with his slightly off-color stories. As I listened, I watched my brother pick off all the best pieces of ham in the pan and my little cousin race Ben's antique model cars on the living room floor, and I could feel us slowly settling into the house, like dropping into a cushy armchair. I realized that a huge part of making a home your own comes with the sharing of the space with those you love.

In the weeks after we moved in, while the walls filled quickly with art and family photos, the rooms re-

TOP and MIDDLE: Ice cream sundaes and cooking out for Napier Easter. | BOTTOM: Some of my family on Easter Sunday.

mained sparsely furnished because I wouldn't put just anything in there: I had resolved to buy only pieces that would be heirlooms someday. I would find antiques we could afford or have Ben build the perfect pieces to hold the things that mattered to us. No more throwaway furniture that was trendy for a season.

I found a 1920s mission-style oak buffet in an antiques mall near Meridian that was thankfully in our price range because of a stain on the top, which I covered with a simple clay vase filled with dried lavender. We used a warped butcher block, heavy as lead, as a landing place at the end of the sofa for books about Laurel. My parents' enormous corduroy sofa became ours. The fabric was out of style but the silhouette was timeless, so we

had it slipcovered in heavy, washed white denim.

One morning, I looked at the fireplace and did not think of the wedding that had taken place at its hearth in the 1940s. Instead, I imagined how nice it would look with our Christmas stockings hanging there, embroidered with our names.

Months passed and summer arrived, and one Sunday afternoon, I felt in my bones that we were home. The rain held off long enough for us to go to church and come home for lunch. But before long, the sky became darker than felt natural and the rain came back ten times heavier than before. I was lying on one couch, Ben on the other, drifting into and out of sleep.

The house was silent and insulated; I could only hear rain, quiet thunder, and, every hour, the church bells playing hymns a block away. While I

lay there listening to the muffled sounds outside the window, I burned a candle I used only in the springtime, and the smell was all around me. It reminds me of sweet olive, walking to work, coming home to make a fresh vegetable supper, sunburned cheeks. I closed my eyes and drifted off: reluctant to miss the moment but thankful for rest.

Our house had begun to feel like family even though it was only an assemblage of wood, brick, and glass. Our pajamas lived there and our favorite thick socks, our coffee and our pillows and our cars that we named. The inexpensive Persian rug we had found on the floor of an antiques store in Roanoke, the books bought secondhand, the cotton tote from Square Books.

They all lived there with us, punctuating our lives and our days. Black-and-white photos of our grandparents and great-grandparents, young, laughing, riding bicycles, holding hands in the ocean, proudly displaying caught blue crabs on a faraway dock, posing with a giant watermelon, holding puppies that were long ago history, everywhere in our house. On the bookshelves, on the walls, hanging beneath the dimly lit sconces, reminding us that life goes on and they're still here, in us. At home.

As with any great story, we've never wanted it to end.

A Friend, or Two

Ben and I knew we wanted to find our first family dog to guard—and play in—our first fenced-in yard. We've loved Great Pyrenees since we met a handsome one on the Oxford Square during our days at Ole Miss. Sometime during the renovations we picked up the Mississippi Market Bulletin, *a weekly classified for agriculture: tractors, trailers, chickens, bulls, and farm dogs. Inside we found a listing for a solid white Great Pyrenees mix, a six-month-old puppy who was already the size of a full-grown Labrador. Ben brought him home, and while we worked on renovating, he became the guardian of the house. Though he was almost as big as a full-grown retriever, he was so shy he wouldn't come to us for the whole first week. We named him Chevy, as in Chevrolet.*

One stormy night we were on the way back to the house after picking up another fast-food supper in between installing the living room ceiling fan and the kitchen sink. As we turned onto our new street, I spotted the inviting glow of our cottage from the lights we'd installed in the flower beds. Our American flag was lit up,

---

LEFT: The living room. *Photo by Jean Allsopp* | RIGHT: Chevy was a huge puppy.

TOP LEFT: Making spaghetti and meatballs, my favorite meal. | TOP RIGHT: Meals on the porch became our daily ritual.
BOTTOM LEFT: The light in the dining room made it my favorite place to paint. | BOTTOM RIGHT: He never makes it through a chapter.

Our household began to feel like family even though it was only an assemblage of wood, brick & glass.

There has been some sort of ongoing project on our home since the day we bought it. As I write this, we are updating and adding on to our master bathroom. In that process we found a hammer inside the wall from when the house was built. That very day, the granddaughter of Dr. Haynes, the original owner, knocked on our door. She gave us photographs of when it was first built, which we framed alongside the hammer. We could not have planned something that so captures the past and future coming together, finding a way to make something good out of all of it.

and the new wreath, dried boxwood, hung on the door. We pulled into the carport and walked through our quiet, empty house to the back door. I saw that Chevy was nestled, safe and sound, in the doghouse Ben had built. He knew he was home.

A few months later a full-blooded, fully grown Great Pyrenees wandered up to Mammaw's house in the country. The dog had been eating out of her trash and the few scraps she threw him every day. His bushy white fur was matted and full of spurs, ticks, and fleas, and he was starving—underweight but still huge. We assumed he lived on a neighboring farm, but as days turned to weeks, it became clear that he was homeless.

Over Valentine's Day weekend, Ben and Jim took the pickup over there, loaded the dog up, and brought him home, giving Chevy a much bigger, lazier brother to help him guard our new backyard. We cleaned him up and named him Baker, as in Studebaker.

So we had two dogs named for two old cars. At first Chevy and Baker weren't too keen on each other; then they became friendly; then they became brothers and mascots of the neighborhood: the two polar bear dogs of Laurel.

In Mississippi, the rain can last for days. During a wet spell that first summer, the dogs were stranded in the workshop, their only dry island. They had been asleep in there for about three days straight, aside from a few minutes spent boredly pacing the porch, hoping the rain would stop if they got close enough to the drops trickling from the eaves.

Baker has always been cripplingly afraid of loud noises. When New Year's Eve or the Fourth of

July rolls around, Chevy is the dutiful little brother who lies beside him while his brother plays dead. Soon enough we found that a corn dog will bring him back to life.

One day Ben and I were both at work when an unexpected storm rolled up and we had not opened the garage door for Baker. I got a phone call from the Laurel chief of police, Tyrone.

"Erin, is Baker out?" he asked.

As I sat at my desk at work, my heart racing, I said, "Not that I am aware of."

Baker had heard a roll of thunder and made a break for it—he had escaped the fence, and a Laurel police officer had spotted him running to our vet's clinic a few blocks away. The officer had given him a police escort to the clinic door, and Tyrone gave us a call.

Such things can happen only in a small town.

LEFT: Baker and Chevy, Fat and Little. | RIGHT: Family history in the entryway. *Photo by Jean Allsopp*

TOP LEFT: The dining room with the oak buffet. *Photo by Jean Allsopp* | TOP RIGHT: Half bathroom we added a couple years after moving in.
BOTTOM LEFT: The kitchen. *Photo by Jean Allsopp* | BOTTOM RIGHT: Our bedroom and the armoire Ben built. *Photo by Jean Allsopp*

Before TV, my old blue Chevy was synonymous with my "Vote Big Ben" campaign around Laurel.
I ran as an independent.

13

A Departure

Ben

Owning a piece of property and the historic house that sat on it, and having a business in downtown Laurel, made us feel more connected to the City Beautiful.

We were finally feeling like true adults, which made what would've been a crazy-sounding idea just a few years earlier seem not only sensible but preordained.

One night in 2013, Jim and Mallorie, who now lived in a house down the street, invited us over for dinner. Though downtown was becoming slightly more of a destination, it didn't have many options for any food after 2 p.m., so we often ate at each other's houses. Along with Josh and Emily, we were all members of Laurel Main Street, which had gone from a fledgling organization—more an idea than anything else—to a leader of economic development in our city.

Our goal had been to make the city a place young people would want to move to, where new parents would want to raise children, and where businesses would want to set up shop. An army of volunteers raised thousands of dollars a year for his-toric preservation in Laurel and triggered a downtown revival that continues to this day.

Jim, Mallorie, Erin, and I were having dinner out on their front porch and got to talking, as we often did, about our city and all its issues and brainstorming ideas. Jim seemed more revved up than usual, talking about how it was time for some young blood to get involved with city government. "Somebody new needs to run for city council," he said. "Win or lose, it's time to shake things up."

I told him I agreed and had been kicking the idea around in my head, too.

"Well, you should do it," he said. "If not, I just might."

The city council seat for Ward 5 in Laurel was held by a twenty-four-year incumbent. He wasn't a bad person and he didn't have bad intentions, but, as I had heard from many people in town, two decades in office had left him too comfortable in that seat. Meanwhile, the streetlights in our neighborhood had died and never come back to life, the potholes were big enough to swallow cars, and anyone who pulled off the highway into Laurel would have no idea they had entered a beautiful and historic Mississippi town. As I saw it, our city councilman just sat contentedly in his seat, waiting for the next election to fall into his lap.

I agreed with Jim that someone needed to challenge him for the privilege of leading our town—and after some soul-searching, I realized I had it in me to take it on. A few months after that dinner, I an-

My official campaign headshot, taken by my official campaign graphic designer/photographer, Erin Napier.

nounced my run for city council. Jim was right: the town needed not only young blood on the ticket but younger people at the ballot box, too. I felt as though, with passion and effort, I could bring them out.

"If you aren't confident you can win," my grandfather, who had a long career in politics, told me, "you shouldn't bother running." I agreed, so I spent the next seven months working as hard as I could, sacrificing time with the youth ministry, with family, with working on the house, and with everything else to make it happen. I raised money, went to every event that would have me, knocked on every door, and enlisted volunteers from every corner of the ward to help me put up yard signs and get the word out. Whatever it took to be fully present in my ward and get to know my constituents, I was all in.

It was an uphill battle on a few fronts. For one, the ward was 84 percent minority, and here I was, a twenty-nine-year-old white boy no one knew, trying to win votes. Also, I ran as an independent and insisted on having both Republican and Democratic advisers on my team.

Plus, though I had lived in Laurel for five years and was the mascot at the Loblolly Festival, I was still an out-of-towner. Though I felt as though that gave me a fresh perspective and the zeal of a convert, you can't go around saying such things in a small town. The outsider card must be played carefully because small-town people, especially in the South, are very territorial. There were a great number of Laurel voters who were older, set in their ways, and had never been anywhere else. The last thing they wanted to hear about was someone from elsewhere telling them how things should be. They had issues with the town and were happy to voice those issues, but it felt like many of them didn't want to do any-

thing about them. But I stayed positive, trying to view myself as a vessel.

When meeting with them, I tried to tap into God's perfect ratio: two ears and one mouth. Something I learned was that most of them didn't want to hear my ideas or my promises. They wanted me to listen, so I obliged. I heard stories of corruption, of civic laziness, of a community looking for a change, of citizens frustrated or fed up or throwing in the towel.

A little old lady on 1st Avenue said she had been trying to get the trees that rose up from the grass patch past her sidewalk trimmed for the last few years. It was a safety issue for her, because she felt it isolated her house in a way that could be dangerous. When I sat down with her, she didn't mince words. "I'll tell you what," she said. "I'll vote for you, but that tree better be trimmed your first week."

"Absolutely," I said.

Unfortunately, a couple of weeks after that conversation, someone from the city came over and cut the tree.

I learned about neighborhood conflicts and politics, waste, drainage systems, traffic patterns, schools and taxes, and how many cars you can park on your lawn—it was an education.

I carried a little blue notebook in my shirt pocket, a trick I'd learned from my granddaddy, a local politician who had worked on state-level campaigns. When I started campaigning, he told me to always write down people's names and their concerns as you heard them, along with any facts that would help you

ABOVE: There were other clever sayings, too. Like "Big Ben Means Business in Ward 5."

The little blue campaign notebook.

remember them, as in "had little boy playing basketball in driveway" or "loves the New Orleans Saints."

We used anything and everything we could to get my name out there: "Vote Big Ben!" became our regular salutation. And of course I had a ringer on my staff: I was married to my own personal graphic design firm. Erin made sure nobody's campaign material looked as good as mine. My face and name were plastered on twenty-foot-tall banners on buildings all over the surrounding neighborhoods. Even I got sick of my face.

Though I didn't share it with anybody, I viewed the city council as a springboard. My plan was to win the seat through a mix of hustle and charm, shake things up at city hall, and, after a couple of terms, become mayor. Maybe it was an outsized idea, but I thought I could pull it off. I loved the town as only an outsider could and felt I could help it reach its potential.

Ward 5 encompassed half of the historic district, just about all of downtown, and two of the major entrances and exits into Laurel from the interstate, which were beat down and unseemly looking. That was the face we were showing to the world, the first impression visitors got of our town.

There also was no effort being made to recruit

new businesses to our area. We felt as though with LMS we had done work to revitalize downtown, but there was only so much we could do without having someone in a position of government to help grow our community and be a spokesperson for those issues.

In June, on the eve of the election, I wrote an op-ed for the local newspaper, my way of leaving it all on the field. I opened up about how it broke my heart that so many descriptions of our town began with the past, as in "Laurel was once" and "Laurel used to be." There was a glut of defeatism that was sinking us.

I talked about the need to merge the old with the new, the historical with the technological, the classic with the modern, how celebrating the past can be a springboard to the future. Erin and I had designed our homes that way, and her business had flourished because of it. Laurel felt ripe for the exact same principle: the perfect marriage of new and old. It was a place with a rich history that was just left to sit on the vine. Why have something old if you're not going to use it and take care of it? I ended by proclaiming that I was proud of what our town had once been but, more important, excited about what it could be.

It gives me chills to read that op-ed today because I did not know that my resolve and commit-

ment to the town would pay off in a big way a couple of years later.

One guy in his twenties I became friendly with used to strike up conversations with me all the time, agreeing with my proposals, promising he'd vote for me. "It's time for some change," he'd say, going on and on about our current councilman's faults.

On election day he showed up with his head down and said, "Ben, can I talk to you?"

"Sure thing. What's up?"

"I know I told you that I was gonna vote for you, but actually"—he lowered his voice a touch—"I'm a felon. And I can't vote. I'm sorry."

"That's all right," I said. "Don't worry about it." I thought it showed true class that he was honest with me about it.

"But I brought five people with me," he said, "and they voted for you."

I thanked him for his help and walked away with the distinct impression that I was going to win. Even the votes I didn't get were leading to votes!

Later that day we cast our vote, went down to the courthouse with my family and friends, and anxiously awaited the returns.

I lost, with 40 percent of the vote.

My granddaddy had told me to have enough confidence to think I was going to win, but maybe I'd had too much. My challenger had nearly lost his

ABOVE: My graphic designer showing off her work.

primary, so I might have had a false sense of security. Plus I had wrapped my head around the idea of representing my beloved town to such a degree that it hadn't really occurred to me that I might lose.

For more than half a year, I had given myself to that campaign—everything I had and some I didn't know I had. When the results came in, I swallowed my tears and my pride as people shook my hand and just tried to get to my truck to get us home. People understood that I was disappointed, but no one knew how devastating it was. I had never given as much of myself to anything, and to have the door shut on me—and publicly—was too much. The experience was hurtful and humbling. It simply did not matter how badly I thought I deserved to win that election, because God has His own plans.

What I hadn't told anyone, not even Erin, was that this was supposed to be my graceful exit from career ministry. It was going to be the next step for me. And I had stumbled out of the gate.

Erin

When the results came in, Ben was uncharacteristically subdued, giving all the volunteers and supporters his thanks and accepting theirs. We went home, and I cried and, as I'd promised myself a few years earlier, tried to find the good in the situation. There was something good worth keeping out of all of it, a blessing even: the campaign had taught us how to work harder than we'd ever worked before. It had pushed and stretched us into people we'd never imagined we could be. Throughout the campaign, I had believed, win or lose, that the experience was a positive thing.

It had also tested us in ways I hadn't expected.

Some mornings I would find an anonymous comment on my journal or Facebook, a stranger letting me know we were failures or someone saying that we were arrogant to think ourselves the saviors of Laurel. I might have inherited my father's confidence, but I am my mother's daughter in matters of the heart—tender as raw biscuit dough.

I knew that I couldn't make everyone in the world like or understand me. I knew that meanness existed, having grown up among it and developed a sense of who I was by protecting myself from it. I was a real person, with real feelings.

The journal had been an effort to brighten my corner of the world. It was not an advice column, a celebrity blog, a news source, or a how-to book. It was an exercise in framing the good and elevating it to a place where it filled the frame, ate up all the

ABOVE: The moment the election results were announced, sitting in the courthouse.

Mmmm mm mmmm mmm... Pity Cake! DELICIOUS!

We bought an ice cream cake at Dairy Queen and took it to Jim and Mallorie's office because we felt sorry for ourselves the day after the loss. We tried to eat it, but it was frozen solid and broke the plastic spoons. Figures, don't it?

negative space. On its best days, it was a community for people like me who loved pancakes, old things, Jesus, and long conversations on long walks.

In my work for Laurel Main Street in those years, I carried that approach outward, into the town I love. If there was an ugly, dilapidated facade with absentee owners, I would design a beautiful banner to cover it up. If there was a big blank wall facing a thoroughfare through downtown, I would design a kitschy "Visit Laurel" ghost sign that felt as though it had always been there.

I had always believed that it's your responsibility to better your community, however you can. That's what I had tried to do, and by running for office, that's what Ben had wanted to do. Whether he succeeded or not just didn't seem to be the point. If you could meet a need by simply giving a piece of yourself, how could you not try?

Ben

When I tried to return to my regular life with the youth ministry, I realized pretty quickly that it wasn't possible. A crack had developed in my facade, and spending all that time on the campaign had made it spread until it became too visible to ignore. I'd been struggling with my future in the ministry for years, but returning to it after the campaign made it plain: I didn't belong there.

Gene Horton, one of my pastors, once said to me, "You shouldn't do it unless you have to." If you aren't absolutely called to the ministry, if you can live without it, then it isn't the right place to be. I had known that, but I'd never allowed myself to go there mentally. Until one day, when I started buying into the reality of *I'm going to do this for the rest of my life*, I felt a quiet panic take over.

I was thirty years old: the time to start on a new course was running out. I was ready to move on and be what I was supposed to be, but God's plan wasn't clear to me anymore and I was scrambling. So I held that doubt inside, covered and protected. I felt it was my duty not to let my wife see how big the crack had become.

Cautiously, I mentioned to Erin one day that I felt myself aging out of youth ministry. Despite my effort to keep it low-key I know it scared her, so I let it drop. I have always carried a chivalrous sense of marriage. Making sure my wife didn't have to worry about me remained one of the key precepts, but this is what keeps our marriage strong: we tell each other everything.

On a hot summer night in 2014 in the court-yard of an old tavern in St. Augustine, I sat watching Erin draw the place, the way she would do houses on *Home Town* years later. It had been about a year since the election, and I was having something of a crisis of confidence about what to do with myself.

She looked up, coming out of her focus as though she was noticing the rest of the world for the first time. And she turned to me. "What's wrong, babe?" she asked. "You're acting weird."

She was reaching for a door that I'd kept shut for a long time. She's always been an intuitive person, and it's likely she sensed that it was about to burst open. Once I gave way, it all came pouring out. Chivalry be damned: I knew I'd married a woman who could handle it.

Erin sketching before we had the talk.

The night I told her I didn't know what I was going to do next, we walked all over St. Augustine hand in hand. Same team, as always.

That night as we walked through the darkened streets of America's oldest city, my wife distracted me with stories about her childhood there, flirted with me in alleys, took my hand, and led me to my favorite gelato shop.

It's not that she wasn't scared, too; she was, but this is how we hold each other up: when we are afraid of the dark, one will pretend to be brave in order to lead us both back into the light.

At thirty years old, I was explaining to my wife, the woman I'd sworn to provide for and protect, that I didn't know what I was going to be when I grew up. I couldn't keep doing what I was doing; it wasn't right to work in ministry when my heart wasn't committed to it anymore.

"The election was my way out," I said. "Now I don't know what to do with myself."

The hairline crack in my foundation had become a canyon: it was a mile wide and now lay out in front of her.

Anytime Erin is upset, I make her tell me everything. That simple act of getting it out of her head and into the world helps her to see the situation more clearly. It gives her the language and the perspective to absorb the big picture.

That summer, we flipped our roles. She smiled at me with those beautiful green eyes. "We're on vacation, Big," she said. "Don't worry about that now. We'll figure it out." Then she reached over, putting her hand on mine.

I talked to my parents, who, as ministers, brought a level of empathy that helped clear away some of the fog. I'm extremely passionate about my faith, but as a career felt as though I were cheating at it.

One day in June, Josh asked me if I wanted to get lunch. The conversation was the same as always: How's work going? How's the church? You reading anything new? I'm looking for a part for this vehicle, seen anything like it on Craigslist? Then the conversation turned; as he'd known me for so long, I imagine Josh sensed a storm rumbling inside of me, even in our casual talk.

"Look," Josh said, "I know you're worried, but I think it's pretty obvious what you're supposed to do."

"Oh, yeah?" Josh is wise, but I couldn't imagine that he had the solution. I heard him out, though.

"Sure," he said, as though it were the most obvi-

ABOVE: A photo I took of Erin about thirty minutes before I dropped the existential bomb on her.

Harry Met Sally, when Harry runs to a New Year's Eve party because he has to tell Sally "I came here tonight because when you realize you want to spend the rest of your life with somebody, you want the rest of your life to start as soon as possible."

So I went straight to Erin's office and told her I knew what was next. She immediately felt at peace about it and knew what I knew. Everything had been coming together to bring me to this next step. God had been telling me for a long time what I needed to do, but He wanted me to act according to His timing.

There was a relief to my decision but heartache as well: I was leaving behind the students in the youth program with whom I had become close. I loved working with them, teaching them about faith at a point in their lives when everything feels so elevated, so hard, and so confusing. Moments of witnessing kids experience revelations about their faith or when they've been questioning something and the answer finds them and they just light up—those times encapsulated what I loved about the work.

ous thing in the world. "Erin needs help at work, and you've been looking for someone to work part-time with her. Why couldn't that be you? And you could build furniture on the side and sell it."

I was about to respond, knock it down, when I realized I had no rebuttal. He was exactly right. It was a moment of clarity I hadn't experienced since the night I'd told Erin that I would marry her one day.

I had thought about building furniture to make a living, but that's a tough thing to start from scratch. I also knew that handling the business end of Lucky Luxe was sucking the creativity out of Erin. For some reason, Josh's way of putting it all just made sense.

There's a great line I remembered from *When*

But as I aged, it felt more and more as though I were jamming a square peg into a round hole. Over the course of a decade, I'd worked in some capacity with hundreds of youth ministers, and none of them seemed like me. There were youth ministers in their forties who were clicking with the teenagers on a different level; maybe because they were parents and had circled back to relating to that age group in a new and powerful way. They developed lessons and sermons that connected with the students where they were, not where they wished they would be. Then there were the awkward postmidlife types who were still trying to be young and hip, and their approach seemed superficial.

ABOVE: Our first portrait together as mom-and-pop shop owners. *Photo by Brooke Davis*

I'd worked with some incredible leaders who knew they were doing important work for the body of Christ, whether they had two hundred teenagers in their youth program or two. And I'd met some ministers who'd bragged about the numbers of kids attending their meetings, as if those souls were statistics they were putting up on the board. Did they believe that *they* had brought those kids to Christ or that God had? No matter which direction I looked, I didn't see myself in the ministry, and so I couldn't see a future for myself there.

By the fall, a few things made it easier to leave. There were a couple of confrontations with parents that made me feel sure it was time to make my move. One parent went out of his way to insult me in front of the students, saying mine wasn't a real job, and that I gave more attention to my wife than to the kids. It felt like an affirmation to me because it was true: I would always put my family before my students.

I thought about my dad a lot during that time. How in his forties with four children and a wife he had gone back to school to follow his calling as a minister. It had been a waking-up-in-the-ditch moment, and he'd had to do it. My ditch moment was the opposite: leaving a career in the church.

I decided I would give a three-month notice, as finding a new student minister was an arduous process. I wrote my letter of resignation, let Erin and my parents proofread it, then printed it off and sealed it in an envelope. I called Mark, the head pastor at our church, and asked if he could come over for coffee the next morning. We've been friends and colleagues for many years, and I think he knew before I could even tell him.

You can't change the DNA in something. You can't squeeze a big-block V8 engine into a Beetle, you can't put someone like Erin into a corporate job, you can't force someone like me—even with my strong faith—to spend my life in the ministry. There has to be respect for what someone or something is, or else growth isn't possible.

I felt so alone, but I soon realized I wasn't. Because of Erin's journal, many people—some of whom I didn't know—learned of my decision. Those who were working in the church or in other fields they'd lost their passion for messaged me to tell me that I had helped inspire them to pursue their dreams. It was an unintentional result, but it helped me feel more grounded in my choice. I was one among so many others. In the years to come, I'd be rewarded by my decision in ways I could never have imagined, finding ways to minister to the people around me regardless of my profession.

At the time, of course, I couldn't have known that. I only knew I had to follow my heart because otherwise I was lying to myself. I wanted to be able to look in the mirror every morning and know for certain that I was doing what God intended for me, something that brought out the best in me.

Sick days became regular occurences by 2012. I spent so many days half asleep, feverish, on the couch.

14

A Crisis

Erin

Our house, finally as finished as an old house can be, had become part of my heart and soul.

I loved its creaky spot in the hallway, the steep and narrow steps to the bedrooms upstairs, how you could smell clean laundry from the front door and the rooms held on to the scent of garlic and bacon for hours after dinner.

I loved that my grandmother's quilts had a place in the linen closet and the painting of my daddy's old hunting dog, Champ, had a place on the picture rails.

I loved the little lamp in the kitchen that invited guests for a midnight snack, the deep porch that wrapped around the corner to the French doors where we would eat last-minute dinners with my family in the springtime.

I loved the way it comforted me after a long day, from the moment I dropped my bag on the landing.

It was the kind of place that felt friendly even on a rotten day. Above all, I loved that Ben lived there. We felt lucky for everything we had, but I

felt an itch I could not scratch. I wanted to take on a new adventure, travel, seek something I couldn't quite name.

For years I'd dreamed of going to Italy. I'd imagine sitting with Ben in the backseat of a tiny car on a narrow street, my fingers sticky with gelato, our driver telling us stories we couldn't understand. We would taste the freshest tomatoes in the world and dip warm, chewy bread in olive oil. My sandaled feet would be gritty and filthy from walking all over Florence, and I would stop to buy a beautiful leather bag from a street vendor in Sorrento. We would stay in a little villa in the country at the end of a winding dirt road bordered with spindly cypress trees. Late in the day, maybe after a nap, we'd swim in the turquoise water of Cinque Terre.

Lying in bed together, Ben and I lazily daydreamed and scrolled through Airbnb villas and apartments up and down the boot. We made a plan. And one day in February 2014, I sat down at my computer and booked it. The plane tickets, the villas, the sticky gelato hands. We were going to Italy.

But my body had other plans.

The next morning, I woke up early in the quiet dark with a sinister, low-grade gnawing ache up high in my belly. It had returned. It had been many months since its last appearance, but when it came, it was always like this, waking me from a dead sleep.

The first time it happened, I was a sophomore in college. Ben and I had been dating for a few months, and we had invited our friends over to my parents' house, where Mama made breakfast for supper, a sausage, egg, and cheese casserole. I could not stop myself from having seconds, then thirds.

In the dead of night, sleeping in my childhood bed, I woke up as a dull ache rose from the bottom of my rib cage. I twisted and writhed in the sheets, swearing I would never eat breakfast casserole again, trying to contort my body into a comfortable position. But the pain would not dissipate. By the next day, as mysteriously as it had arrived, it vanished. That would happen once a year, maybe twice, and I always wrote it off as an unusual stomachache, painful but not altogether out of the ordinary.

A few years later, not too long after Ben and I got married, the spells became regular. With each bout, I would engage in a routine of self-medicating—heat, cold, diet, over-the-counter remedies—and hoping the pain would pass. One morning I woke Ben up and told him we needed to go to the hospital. We drove through the cloud of hot steam rising from the parking lot grates near the entrance. A shiver ran down my arms.

At 6 a.m., the cafeteria breakfast smells drifted through the air-conditioning into the mostly empty waiting room, creating a nauseating odor of food, antiseptic, and sanitized laundry. I began to shake and realized I had a fever coming on.

My belly was bloated like a whiskey barrel, even though my stomach was empty because I'd had no appetite for days. My skin felt like sausage inside its casing, and I envisioned it ripping down my sides and bursting if I moved too much.

After hours of tests and bloodwork and painkillers injected directly into my bloodstream, the doctor let me go, awash in a sweet numbness that spread from my toes to the ends of my hair. They

ABOVE: I tried eating oatmeal the morning after I had booked the trip to Italy, but couldn't stomach it.

had found nothing except for a highly elevated white blood cell count; my body was trying to attack something.

And so began many years of searching.

There were many doctors who, after tests and scans, gave me false hope with various diagnoses that didn't pan out. Each time, I was like a child, believing their every word, thankful to have some kind of answer on the way. But they all came up empty. All that we found were discarded theories about my gallbladder, celiac disease, abdominal migraines, ulcers, intestinal parasites, and a doctor who suggested that it was all in my mind.

"You're getting anxious and creating these symptoms," he said. "I'd like you to try this."

Out of desperation, I took the tiny proffered pill and had a bizarre sensation of fire washing over my body in waves. The blank look on my face the next day scared both me and Ben, and I never tried it again. Another failed diagnosis was porphyria, a rare blood disorder, which I terrified myself with by googling.

The worst attack I ever had was during a youth group trip to North Carolina with Ben's students. I thrashed helplessly in a rustic motel bed for three days, soaked with fever, shivering, in so much pain I could hardly breathe.

I had never reached that point of hopelessness before, wondering if it would ever end or if it would just kill me. More than the pain was the worry of not knowing. A creative mind goes both ways, and I imagined a cancer eating away at me little by little, an unnamed gray area spreading across the healthy pink.

During Ben's run for city council, I'd had a series of attacks. While he was on the high school stage for his first debate, I was on my knees in the bathroom in a silk dress and high heels throwing up, unable to stand or walk, a flattering new side effect of the stronger painkillers dispensed to me in the ER. On the ride home I couldn't stop my tears from falling as I watched the neighborhood go by through the open window, the breeze keeping me from heaving again.

Then the illness started to take up more space. It expanded outward from my body into other areas of my life. I began to feel pangs of disinterest in Lucky Luxe, a kind of sapped enthusiasm that frightened me. I had built my professional future on something that somehow, quietly, did not feel like my passion anymore.

Our friends were all long married, and weddings had lost their magic for me. Designing a piece of paper announcing a single day suddenly felt inconsequential. Impermanent. I began to wonder if the work I was pouring my heart into was silly, clutter to be discarded once the information was recorded on a calendar. I noticed more and more shops on the Internet peddling similar products and recognized that the competition was likely the reason business had been slow.

ABOVE: Once, I had to swallow a pill camera that would record my intestines. Fun!

About a year before, I found a creative windfall after seeing the trailer for Baz Luhrmann's version of *The Great Gatsby* and Ben suggested that I design a wedding invitation suite inspired by 1920s Art Deco. The streamlined, chic fonts and gilded, geometric, glamorous motifs of the era were ripe for inspiring formal weddings, and for many months after that movie, it seemed that was all anyone wanted. I had gotten lucky by designing the "next big thing" ahead of the curve once again, just like the hankies that started it all. I let the green light from F. Scott Fitzgerald's novel and the gold-foiled extravagance of Jay Gatsby's parties lead the way creatively, leaving the dark corners of the story out of frame.

The invitations were hugely popular, to the point that even years later, I was selling Gatsby as fast as we could churn them out—and little else.

But because my creativity went on autopilot for such a long while as Gatsby took care of us, I felt doubt about my design and business savvy creeping in even though I had made something good—in my work and in my life. That should have been enough, shouldn't it?

One thing I kept putting off was talking in earnest about all this with God. It's easy to feel like an ungrateful, petulant child if you get serious with God only when life gets scary. I suppose that's why I put it off.

One night I lay awake, unable to get this off my mind. Distracted by my own moping and nowhere close to sleep, I picked up my old standby, *Streams in the Desert,* the devotional book that had given me the courage to leave my day job in the first place. I turned to that day's entry:

It would not be in our best interest to always remain in one happy and comfortable location. . . .

But take heart! It could never be better to stay once He determines otherwise; if the loving hand of our Lord moves us forward, it must be best.

The words made my breath catch. When I got back into bed, I picked up my phone and began mindlessly scrolling through Instagram. My finger stopped when I saw a devotional an old friend had posted:

Instead of letting difficulties draw you into worrying, try to view them as setting the scene for My glorious intervention. Keep your eyes and your mind wide open to all that I am doing in your life.

I couldn't ignore the signs. With Ben snoring beside me, I turned out the lamp and crept into the hallway. Feeling a little silly—but mostly as though I'd run out of options—I sat down on the rug, like a kindergartner. It was unnatural and I felt self-conscious, but in the dark with just the sound of the heat humming quietly, I started praying.

It was not the quick casual prayer I'd been getting by with lately. This was real, hard prayer. It was stiff at first. But it's that way sometimes when you've been away for a while; you don't know how to break the ice with an old friend. I started talking, really talking, and then I couldn't stop myself. I prayed for a long time: for healing from my sickness; for renewed love for my work; for Ben, who was bearing the burden for both of us; for my worried parents, who hid their worry so well for my sake.

It came out casually, then intimately. I asked Him to be with me, to show me the way, to light my path and guide me. In the dark and quiet, He transformed everything. It all became a challenge bound to elevate me, not a problem doomed to shatter me.

I got up, exhausted, and went to bed for a long, dreamless sleep.

From that point on, I found a place for the good in this, noting every healthy day, choosing to focus on my gratitude that we had survived the year, forcing thoughts of the sickness out of my mind.

So when my eyes opened that February morning in 2014, I felt betrayed. And I knew on top of my doubts about my business, my dream of seeing Italy would remain just that—a dream.

Dr. Roberts had treated me before and always made me feel relaxed—even that morning. She was young, with beautiful red hair, soft-spoken, with a syrupy "Hey, girl, how are you?" style that put me at ease.

But after an ultrasound, I was alarmed. She calmly sat me down and said she wanted to perform an exploratory surgery—the next day. She'd seen something that could have been a tumor or a cyst on one of my ovaries, and the surgeons would have to get in there to determine what it was.

The seriousness and the speed of what was happening were terrifying. I'd been dealing with this illness for years, and no doctor had ever suggested such a drastic step. It was difficult, but I dug in, trying to find the light, hoping for an end to the pain that no one could name.

That evening, Mallorie brought me Rice Krispies Treats for my last meal before surgery. And even though I was terrified of what the next day would bring, it made me smile as I ate the whole pan.

Ben

There's just about nothing harder than standing in the doorway as your wife is being rolled down a hallway, crying and calling your name. It was a horrible and humbling feeling: at six feet, six inches and 300 pounds, I was completely powerless.

I joined Erin's parents as we anxiously waited, expecting a few hours to pass. Part of me was on that cold operating table being put to sleep. But twenty minutes later, Dr. Roberts came into the room and asked to see us. It was too soon. My hands were shaking, and I immediately felt numb. Why were they finished so early? Beside her I noticed Dr. Weber, who had delivered decades of Laurel's babies, whom I wasn't expecting to see.

"ERIN IS VERY SICK,"

Dr. Roberts said. It was as though the volume on her voice had been turned low and the roar in my ears turned up to a deafening level: she explained that they had stopped the operation and would be sending Erin to Jackson for surgery with the best OB/GYN oncological surgeon in the state as soon as he could take her. Oncological: I let the word pinball around my brain for a moment. Cancer?

"Oh, Ben," Erin's mom said, taking my hand. "She's going to be okay." Words of assurance that she believed, even though she didn't know. Parents are good at that. They can tell you something, and you believe them if only because they believe it.

The morning of surgery, our friend Father Jeff, an Episcopal priest, came to the hospital and prayed with my family and me. As he left, I found a semblance of peace as I scanned their faces: my parents, Jim, Mallorie, my brother, Clark, and my aunt Phyllis. And Ben.

After giving me something in my drip to make me less anxious, men in scrubs rolled my bed out of the darkened room. The lights of the hallway were blinding, and I was suddenly aware of how real it all was. I began to cry and call out for Ben.

There were bright spotlights, my doctors' familiar faces half covered in masks. I didn't have enough energy to do anything but lie there and shiver. A gentle voice told me to count backward from ten, that I would fall fast asleep soon. And I counted: *ten, nine, eight, seven . . .*

When the surgeons made the incision and looked into my abdomen, they were shocked: all of my internal organs were completely fused together by bands of scar tissue, making it too risky to proceed with the surgery. Determining that I needed a specialist, they closed me back up immediately. The scar tissue had grown, spread, and formed cocoons throughout my abdomen.

They were unsure if this could be caused by endometriosis, where the uterine lining covers the other organs, or "something else." I was immediately placed on the surgery docket for the next month in Jackson. If it was endometriosis, I was told, my chances of one day bearing children were very unlikely. My mother was devastated, Ben was afraid of the "something else," and I felt myself losing the resolve to be brave. I was being tested, and I struggled to find the strength to remain grateful.

After my surgery, I was rolled into the women's wing, a less scary place with lamps and hardwood floors. Ben slept on the Naugahyde sofa beside me, spilling off the ends without complaint.

Over the next few weeks, I mentally prepared myself for different gradations of what would happen. If I couldn't have children, we would adopt. And even if we couldn't adopt, I would always have Ben. That would be enough.

"You don't have cancer," Dr. Moore said at my consultation a few weeks later. "You're good." He had looked at a decade of my medical records and was effortlessly reassuring. Dr. Moore reminded me of a lovable sitcom star like Michael J. Fox or Jason Bateman. He had an approachable air that made one of the scariest meetings of my life more tolerable. But more than being comforted by his bedside manner, I owe him my life.

In surgery he found the problem, and it was no bigger than a boiled peanut.

Dr. Moore removed a benign cyst from an ovary plus all the scar tissue that had acted like glue, which was binding my internal organs together. Since there would have been no way for things to stretch and grow, it would have kept me from having children. But the scar tissue wasn't the original problem; it was a reaction to something else. The source of the problem was my appendix. It had perforated, meaning it was partially ruptured and encased in a cocoon of scar tissue that had made it appear normal in every CT scan. My appendix had been bursting and healing and bursting and healing itself over and over again for years, leaking into my abdominal cavity. Dr. Moore removed that tiny useless thing that had been the cause of so much pain and was getting ready to kill

ABOVE: Daddy, Mama, and Big waiting with me before the second surgery. They were telling jokes to make me laugh. Daddy had just said, "I think my muscles are getting too big from working out. My pants are too tight."

me. Before we left the hospital, he explained that scar tissue had bound up my organs so badly that it could make it difficult for me to conceive children, even after my appendix was removed. It wasn't likely, but it was a possibility. I was sent home with four incisions on my belly and instructions to take it easy.

By the weekend, I was sitting on our front steps in the sun while Ben washed his truck in the driveway. Everyone was kind and helpful during that time, but without Ben, I don't know where I'd be.

He's as big and strong as a bull, the very physical attributes that can make a girl feel taken care of in a vulnerable state. You don't think about it until you're unable to move naturally—how you need your core muscles to do just about everything. After those surgeries, he picked me up off the sofa, pulled me up from chairs and the bath, helped me get into and out of cars, up and down the stairs, into and out of bed. At the end of the night he would put me into bed and brush off the imagined dust from my feet, just as I have always done at bedtime. We took careful walks and were glad to have made it through the winter with my health on the mend just as the dogwoods were blooming.

ABOVE: I found this pretty Indian caftan before the surgery, and it became my favorite thing to wear post-op.

Oh, what would I do without you?

A couple days after my final surgery, I took this photo after lunch on the porch. Ben had been at a funeral at our church but came home to check on me and help me with lunch. My heart couldn't take how handsome he was that day.

A CRISIS   161

Erin took some photos of me working in the wood shop after Scotsman Co. was off the ground.

15

A Passion

Ben

When I first started building pieces for my family or the house, no matter what I was working on, it always started the same way.

I'd go out to the storage shed and drag everything out into the yard or the carport. Whether it was a custom built-in cabinet or a special gift for Erin, everything had to be taken out of storage and put back. If I didn't finish by the end of the day, I had to put it all back in or secure it somehow because of the unannounced and torrential Mississippi rains. Baker would flop down into the sawdust, his tail sweeping it back and forth, a slobbering, 150-pound dust mop.

One day, Josh came over to borrow some of my saws. He was laying flooring in his office, and there was a warehouse attached to the back of his building where he was going to set everything up. The gears in my head were turning as soon as he told me his ideas for the flooring project.

When you've been working out of a six-by-ten storage building and your friend says he's going to

set up your tools in a 1,400-square-foot warehouse, that's the sound of opportunity knocking. Josh and I worked out a plan for a hobby shop: it would be his building and my tools, and we'd have an equal share of it all to build what we wanted, when we wanted. That was the seedling of what would become my future.

The plan had been for me to help Erin out at Lucky Luxe by removing the burden of business and logistics, and hopefully, it might bring her creativity back to life again. I would also be building and selling furniture on the side to supplement our income. Opening a wood shop was something I had kicked around for a bit and talked to Erin about, but I couldn't quite picture how it would work. I just knew that the more I built pieces of furniture, the more I wanted to do it. And the more I did it, the more I wanted to make it

an important part of my life. The only comparison I could make was when I had met Erin. After spending six days with her, I'd had no doubt in my mind that I wanted to spend all the rest of them with her. Building things with my hands felt right in the same way that being with Erin did.

I believe that the people we love inspire us to be the best versions of ourselves. So as I had witnessed my dad and Erin do, I decided to go all in, carrying little but my faith and my passion. I would put myself out there and see what happened.

In the beginning, my woodworking was very simple. It was like the way an aspiring artist might begin by tracing. I would see something, like the shape of it, and work to make it on my own. It was imitation, learning by simply re-creating something that already existed, like how Erin told me she had painted Vincent van Gogh's *Starry Night* using Q-tips in seventh grade. It would take many pieces, and lots of copying, to go from seeing something in my mind to conjuring it into the world.

The more time I spent building things, the more it felt as though I had grown a new set of eyes. Everywhere I went, I saw antiques I could replicate, remembering the shape of furniture or built-ins to figure out how to make them. I'd be in conversations with people and find I was only half listening because I was staring at a cabinet behind them. That's how it is with a passion: you're thinking about it when you're away from it, even when it's inconvenient to do so. You're just more alive doing it than anything else.

TOP: The wood shop was dank, dark, leaky, and full of musty furniture and taxidermy, Muddy Waters or Sturgill Simpson always on the radio. What I'm saying is, it was perfect.
BOTTOM: Building a fourteen-foot-long dinner table for my parents.

As my pieces got better, I started noticing finishes. I'd always been partial to those old weathered finishes and worked on trying to re-create them with paint, but I learned that it was impossible. You can't age something the way time does. Faded, flaking paint can be created only through years and years of neglect. It is the result of being forgotten, of nature taking its course. That's what creates its beauty.

The more I learned about finishes, the less I liked painted furniture because I wanted to see more of the wood and the story it told. I started learning how to differentiate among wood types, the way the grain comes to life differently depending on how a board was milled. I wanted to know if the lumber was rift sawn or flat sawn or quarter sawn. Once I found a grain of wood I loved, I wanted to learn how to accentuate it, to bring out what was special about it.

I could just go to the hardware store and get a can of stain, but I started investigating: What would happen if I cut that stain and made it thinner? What

if I used a tinted polyurethane? I learned to appreciate the drying speed of water-based finishes but loved the result of the patience required to work with oil-based. How did antique furniture get such a rich, deep tint to it? All my curiosity and trial and error led to a love of reclaimed lumber. The way time ages and tints the wood gives it a more beautiful color than any finish I can mix in my shop.

From there I started noticing the joinery of pieces. I would find myself turning over chairs, climbing under tables, and examining cabinet doors to see exactly how they were held together. I learned about pocket-hole screws and mortise-and-tenon joints. Once I had built a piece of furniture—a kitchen cart—without using screws or nails, only glue and joinery, I felt I'd arrived.

It was a progression, a process of discovery that kept opening up wider and wider.

There's something to be said for finishing up at the end of the day and being able to literally see

ABOVE: My and Josh's first woodshop in the old Johnston Drugs warehouse in downtown Laurel.

what you've made. It's a deeply satisfying feeling to see where those hours went. There are some things you have to work at, but you enjoy doing them so much you don't mind. It doesn't even feel like work. The fact that I wasn't at all good when I started didn't make me love woodworking any less. I got the sense that it was a deep well and I would have to keep lowering myself farther down to get more out of it.

There were entire weeks filled with failure, but I learned to actually enjoy it, to recognize it as a necessary step to getting good.

In the end, I think, you know you love doing something when success and failure are equally valuable. If a project didn't come out the way I expected, I wouldn't stop. I'd break it back down to figure out where I'd gone wrong. I'd look at why the wood had split or see that I should have run the grain a certain way, left a piece a little thicker, or added an extra pin. As Erin had showed me, the good that I got out of some days was not a finished piece at all. It was the experience of and lesson from failing at it miserably.

That doesn't mean I didn't try to bask in the successes, especially if they made someone's life brighter or easier. Our screen door at the back of the house got damaged, and rather than buy one, I took it as an opportunity to build one. Pulling that off emboldened me to build double screen doors for the French doors on the front porch, which Erin had always wanted. I turned her dream of being able to sit with the doors open into a reality, building something that made my wife smile, something that be-

came part of my home, something that came from my hands.

The dining room at my parents' house was too small to accommodate the growing family, so I set about building a new one. I found a fourteen-foot-long old church pew and broke it down, removing the seat and back, then rejoining them for the tabletop. Now my entire family can share a meal together. It was a connective device, the furniture I built, because it brought people together. As I became more adept

ABOVE: We finished staining the dinner table the night before Thanksgiving dinner and brought it into the dining room just in time for the meal.

at using reclaimed materials, the connection became between the past and present (and future) as well.

There's something to be said about the handmade—which is never perfect but holds the stamp of the personal. I'm drawn to it. That's something I've learned about myself as I've gotten older. It's like with music: I like all kinds of music—classic rock, blues, country, bluegrass—but the defining through line is that it's the sound of people making something: the more imperfect (within reason), the more beautiful.

All the while, I was taking on all the business side of Lucky Luxe, allowing Erin to focus on the creative side. It took some time to learn to use a computer like she did, so it was touch and go for a while, but I eventually got the hang of it.

Working together was an extension of the way our lives had been before: she had helped me with the youth ministry, leading small groups when I needed her to and chaperoning on all the trips. In the past, when she'd gotten slammed with work, I'd pitch in here and there. There were very low walls between our two worlds, so the final step of officially working together full-time felt completely natural.

We dreamed of expanding Lucky Luxe into more than a wedding stationery company to pull us

through the slow holiday season when no one gets married. We decided that every year we would add a new product: personal stationery, holiday cards, postcards, candles with scents Erin had designed. As my woodworking became more than a hobby, we started branching out into small things I made, such as cutting boards and rolling pins. Lucky Luxe was growing into something larger than paper and got an additional website to accommodate it: erinandben.co. Erin began collecting vintage and sourcing American-made goods we could sell online in the slow seasons, which, in retrospect, I think was intended as a distraction from her waning interest in stationery.

The next step for me was to take the leap into trying to sell a piece of furniture. The idea came about from our own home. Erin and I had a church pew in our entryway, and one day she casually said, "It would be great if this thing had baskets or drawers." As I tend to do when she has an idea, I got to work: drawing up the plans and making what I called the Elder's Bench—a five-foot church pew with four square drawers underneath it. It had intricate wood-working and joinery in the seat backs with the grain running perpendicular, accentuating its age and coloring.

There was a big beam of quarter-sawn pine with really tight grains that I used for the end cap. The seat bottom was actually from an old bench and was some new-growth yellow pine with knots. The seat back was flat-sawn old heart pine that I cut into strips and jointed together to fill in the back. The drawer frames were more of that same pine, but the drawer facing was Douglas fir. I stained the entire piece with Early American stain that let all of the grain shine but still tied the color of the piece together.

I named my furniture outfit Scotsman Co., after my family heritage. I put the bench up on the web-site, and it sold that day. It was like a validation—not only of the bench but of the entire path I had taken. I had been contributing, but on that day I felt I'd be able to pull my own considerable weight. I've sold a lot of benches since, but none was more important than that first one. I felt like Rocky at the end of his first fight with the champ. I'd gone the distance.

ABOVE: Making rolling pins for erinandben.co.

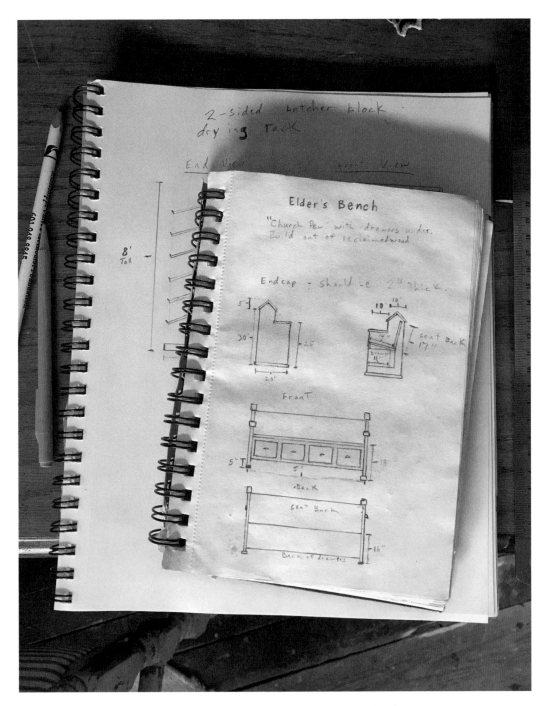

The first drawings of the Elder's Bench from my sketchbook.

The finished Elder's Bench. It was the first piece of furniture I ever sold.

I was so proud of that thing that I wouldn't shut up about it. I had never seen one like it and was one day telling my friend, a veteran builder, about this piece of furniture I'd invented. He politely heard me out.

"Sure, I've seen that before."

"No," I said, correcting him, "but this one has drawers underneath."

"No, I know what you're saying. I've seen it."

"No, but I dreamed this up," I said. "I drew it and made it."

Exasperated, he dug around for a catalog and showed me three companies that made the same thing. "There's nothing new in the furniture world, son," he said. "If it's good design, someone's already done it."

But it didn't matter if I was the first: it felt like I was. It was a beautiful piece of furniture that I had dreamed in my head and then brought to life. It didn't exist in my world, and then it did.

There was a thread running from what I was doing with my days to what I was doing with my life. I had a loose idea of what would make me happy, what kind of life would fulfill me, and then I worked to make it a reality. It took time, but I looked around one day and saw that I had brought that dream to life. I had taken the pieces of my life that I loved, the things that I wanted to hold on to, and used them to create something new.

Once we got brass plates bearing my logo Erin had designed, it was validating. I was really making a go at woodworking.

Press photo for the pilot episode taken for HGTV. *Photo by Brooke Davis*

16

An Opportunity

Erin

In which Lindsey Weidhorn appears.

Subject: FBFF (Future best friend forever)
Hey! I may or may not have been insta stalking you for a bit now. I do that, but it's part of my job. I promise I'm not a creeper. Your life looks amazing and I want to get tape of you and your hubs and your space and your business. I just don't know what the show is . . . Yet. Annnnyways, when are you in NYC?
We need to meet and eat.
L
LINDSEY WEIDHORN
Director, Original Programming & Development
HGTV

In July 2014, two hours after Ben had sealed the envelope of his resignation letter to the ministry, this email showed up in my inbox.

Since the day I had left my corporate job six years earlier, I had been consciously making an effort to "mind the checks," to pay attention to what God was whispering. At the time we had no idea what would come of that random email beamed to us from New York City, but it felt like an affirmation. The timing was that powerful.

Ben and I dived in, realizing that God doesn't always speak in the way we'd assume. Sometimes He speaks in the form of a New York woman in a cat T-shirt who lives for *Gilmore Girls*, cookies, and country music.

She had a contagious verve for life and an untethered way of living it, treating the world as a playground to mess around in. An oddball in the best way possible, Lindsey would be our introduction into the strange and magical world of television.

Lindsey's interest led us to Skype meetings with Jenna and Paul, producers at a production company called RTR Media. TV shows are often made by third-party production companies, not by a network. The companies do a good deal of the legwork: they come up with ideas, find people to carry them out, vet them, get to know them, and then pitch a show idea to the television networks. (If you watch any show, you'll notice in the opening or closing credits various five-second logos for those outside companies.)

Ben and I knew very little about what the producers had in mind other than the renewal happening in downtown Laurel and our renovating old houses. I felt ill equipped to be on TV but passionate enough about Laurel to hopefully make up for it. I tried not to get caught up in an endless stream of what-ifs, as I'm wont to do, and chose to see it simply for what it was: an opportunity to share our family, friends, and town on a very big scale. It was wild and weird. All of a sudden, our small-town life didn't feel so small. It was as though the walls around our little world had been knocked down and there was a whole other universe on the other side that we had never even considered.

A few weeks later, a film crew came down to Laurel to shoot a five-minute promotion clip called a sizzle. The sizzle would be presented to the network, and if the people there liked it, we would go on to the next stage: filming a pilot episode. Then the network would decide if the pilot was good enough to air; the ratings on that would determine if it would be made into a series.

Jenna, Paul, and Lindsey made no false promises, which we appreciated. The door to each phase was extremely narrow, and they told us there was a 2 percent chance that the stars would align and a series would be ordered. If that didn't happen, I wouldn't be crushed. It would have been a gift: of experience, of meeting people, trying something exciting, and learning something new. Worrying about it actually leading to a television show felt greedy: it was so far off our radar that it would have been like getting a call from someone offering us a unicorn and then haggling over the color of its mane.

Locals, caught up in the chance to shine a spotlight on their beloved town, pitched in to rally for Laurel. On social media we asked that people share the things they love about the town—to share a photo of their walk in Gardiner Park or the bricks on 8th Street—and hashtag it #iliveinlaurel. We wanted our love of this place to spread like kudzu. We asked them to invite their out-of-town friends to meet them for Pancake

ABOVE: We did a LOT of Skypes before the show was picked up. A LOT.

Day at the YWCO or for dinner at The Loft. We encouraged them to buy birthday or wedding gifts at Southern Antiques or have a steak cut at The Knight Butcher, instead of spending their money out of town, to show up and cheer for the Tornadoes at the Friday-night game, or to have a milkshake at Phillips Drive-In and pretend they were in *American Graffiti* come to life.

The night before we started shooting, we hosted dinner for the whole crew. The group included Paul, our producer, and David, the director of photography, who right away felt like old friends, perfectly merging into our little circle. The framily all pitched in to make dinner: gumbo, smoked chicken with homemade white BBQ sauce, jambalaya, corn bread, biscuits, green salad with homemade dressing, apple pie, and Aunt Phyllis's famous banana pudding. We ate way too much and stayed up way too late, excited about the adventure about to roll out before us.

Before sunrise the next morning, we met the crew at a dilapidated little house owned by our friend Dr. Wallace. He was about to begin renovations to turn a cottage into a rental and was gracious enough to let us film demolition scenes there, ripping up carpet and smashing walls.

Later we toured a house our friends Grant and Hope were buying for a "real estate day" kind of scene. It was the first time we were wired with body microphones for an entire day, just like the ones they use to make movies and catch mob criminals. It was a strange feeling, knowing that someone was wearing headphones listening to our conversations all day long. There is an itchy feel-

Dinner with the sizzle film crew the night before our two-day shoot.

TOP LEFT: The unnamed sizzle, called simply "Laurel" at the time. | TOP RIGHT: Photos on the hood of Ben's truck. BOTTOM LEFT: Collaborating on a furniture design together. | BOTTOM RIGHT: B-roll fixing a porch floor.

ing when you wear a tiny, forgettable microphone on your body for a day. You consider
your words more carefully because they're
being recorded. It's not like being on the local
news talking about the town festival; it has
an unmistakable feeling of permanence that
takes some getting used to.

Later, we took still photos of me sitting
on the hood of Ben's truck while he leaned
against it, me breathing in his pine sap and
cologne smell. Then we filmed scenes of us
kissing in front of one of the first huge Laurel murals I had designed, of us shopping at
the Rusty Chandelier, of me creating a house
portrait sitting in the kitchen of my studio.

During breaks we watched them film
B-roll—little flashes of idyllic street scenes,
bees landing on flowers, clouds passing over
the city skyline, the train rolling through
town. They give the show a feeling of texture
and atmosphere, a sense of time and place. It
was fascinating, seeing the other side of an
industry we had only ever experienced as a
packaged, polished product from the com-
fort of our sofa. Then we moved to filming in Ben and Josh's
wood shop, where I sketched an idea for a banquette with
storage for the little kitchen we had demoed the day before
and they got shots of Ben clamping and sawing.

Ben and I ended the day settled onto the porch bed for
a three-hour interview about our passions, our talents, our
love for each other, and our town. Our producer Paul, a fun
and freakishly tall young guy with a fading Australian accent,
carried a contagious excitement that rubbed off on everyone.
Talking to him felt as natural as talking to an old friend, except for the expensive camera, its little red blinking light, and
the rest of the crew hovering around us.

The Sizzle Sketches

*Lindsey asked me to submit a
few sketches to HGTV of rooms
I had done from photographs to
be included in the sizzle, and we
ended up making prints of them
to sell.*

ABOVE: Dining Room (watercolor and ink).

Foyer (watercolor and ink).

Kitchen (watercolor and ink).

Watercolor sketches of photos found in the book *Heirloom Modern* by Hollister and Porter Hovey.

Watercolor of photo from the cover of the book *One Man's Folly* by Julia Reed.

Drawing the sketches for the sizzle.

I'll admit it was intimidating at first, measuring my words to avoid clichés, truly explaining my thoughts, but I also reframed it in my mind as a challenge. It forced me to dig deep and talk about the *why* behind my design choice, in the way we'd had to do in art school.

The day ended as it normally would, with dinner on Jim and Mallorie's front porch with the framily. The only two things that made it different were (1) the cameras and (2) that we weren't really having dinner.

The food, scraps, and leftovers from Mallorie's fridge—a cold rotisserie chicken and two-day-old Popeye's biscuits—were props, not for consump-

tion. And it took place at 4:30 in the afternoon, before the sun disappeared, so the light would be right. We lit the lanterns and candles just as we always would, but we positioned our bodies at the table in a most unnatural way, with no one's back to the camera, like Leonardo da Vinci's painting of *The Last Supper*.

I had spent years staging photographs of my invitations in beautiful little vignettes with props and light and objects, and I noticed that staging our bodies or a dinner table set was much the same. You take a situation that happened previously, that has the air and ring of truth, and replicate it.

The conversation and company were just as real as at any framily supper, though, and that's the way it is with the best reality TV. A real moment occurs, and a talented team of people position it so it's well lit and beautiful; there might be a gloss over it, but if the underlying sentiment is true, it rises above the artifice and ends up on film. To show the beauty in the ordinary, you have to turn your head just a little more to the left into the light of the sunset. We have since grown used to it, and styling and packaging our life as it happens has become a fun way of editing the messiness out. In a way, it's a more elaborate extension of the journal I've been keeping all these years, presenting a version of our best selves.

That winter we had a meeting in New York with Lindsey of HGTV and decided to turn it into a family vacation with Jim and Mallorie. We milked

ABOVE: The sizzle dinner scene on Jim and Mal's porch with Josh and Big setting the table (yikes).

Seeds

As a little girl, I would make animal costumes out of papier-mâché and then invent a world for the animals to live in, stories that would unfold in my imagination. The hill behind my house was a mountain; the storm shelter below it, a cave. I would take the seeds of something and plant them and let worlds grow from them. In high school, I would design posters for after-school events and find the seeds that could grow from them. Tasked to create a poster for the French Club, I took the seeds I knew from nineteenth-century France, such as the work of Toulouse-Lautrec, and created a world out of it.

As a professional, designing wedding stationery, I took the seeds of information: the location, the colors, the couple's story and personality. Once again, I was designing a world on a small canvas. Designing homes, even in the beginning, felt like an extension of what I'd always been doing; I was just using different tools, putting down one brush to pick up another. Now I had pillows, wallpaper, shutters, and doors. I was still telling a story and bringing it to life. Though the end products look different, my job has always been to tell people's story in a visual, beautiful way, to use color and form and objects to explain their journey. It isn't graphic design or interior design; it's all storytelling. I don't separate the two.

every minute of it: seeing the Rockettes at Radio City Music Hall, riding the subway to Caffe Roma for cannoli, seeing the Christmas windows at Saks, visiting Martha Stewart headquarters, and going to a New York Giants game. Mallorie and I bemoaned our crippled feet after walking the city in heeled boots, while Ben and Jim turned every stop into a party. At Minetta Tavern on our last night, I couldn't get Ben to leave. After closing down the restaurant and paying our tab, I found him swinging a bell behind the bar, bellowing "Merry Christmas!" for his new friends on the waitstaff, who said he looked like a young Santa Claus.

The next day, we made the drive north to our favorite town in western Massachusetts, Stockbridge. We spent the days exploring the snowy countryside, finding tiny cemeteries hidden in thickets of snow, a Shaker community with red barns that reminded me of the puzzles I had put together with my grandmother while growing up. We ate pancakes beside fireplaces that cracked and popped and made us feel warm in our bones, feeling grateful for a few days of the most idyllic winter magic.

ABOVE: Me, Big, Jim, and Mallorie at Radio City Music Hall in NYC.

A snowy day in Stockbridge, Massachusetts.

I think back on that trip as the last days of a certain type of normalcy. In a rented car on the way to LaGuardia Airport with Mal and Jim, we got a call from Lindsey saying our pilot had been ordered. Our lives were about to take an enormous left turn, with huge learning curves ahead, and we would be jumping into new things feetfirst without really knowing what we were doing. But then, that's life for everyone, isn't it?

Ben

In March 2015, the producers wanted to give a message to the network in New York about Laurel: "This place is real." Of course, I knew that Laurel was special, always have. But it warmed my heart hearing that an outsider thought so, too.

We went full steam ahead, scheduled to start shooting the pilot in May. The director came to town in late March, when the days in Mississippi are already pretty hot. We showed him around, fed him well, introduced him to the locals, and toured some houses that needed a little love: in short, we showed him the best that Laurel had to offer.

In the months before filming we had to make our simple lives camera ready. Of course, the idea was that we were showcasing who we were and the town we loved, but TV magic just doesn't happen by itself. The first thing I turned to was my pickup truck, which I had always imagined with a company logo on the side. It's a light blue 1962 Chevrolet C-10, a name that, to me, naturally translated to Clint; it evoked my childlike impression of Clint Eastwood, the toughest man around besides my daddy. I asked a local sign painter, Will Sellers, to do a hand-painted logo—

Scotsman Co.—in white script across the side. With a few strokes of his brush, Clint was transformed into a company truck.

The next stop was the wood shop, which was really just a dank warehouse in a basement of exposed brick. The shop was a beloved space with tons of character, but it was also a rough and leaky place. It had few legitimate power sources, dangerous access through a narrow door and down a flight of stairs, and a collection of cheap and hand-me-down tools. Josh and I had stretched extension cords from the store space in the front of the building, and a single droplight had been strung up and over a rafter. So we got some new equipment and ran some new power, brought the space up to code, cleaned it up, and added new lights. Scotsman Co. was ready for its close-up. I also helped get Lucky Luxe ready for her big debut, with some custom wainscoting and a standing desk to make it look more like an office than our old home.

* * *

ABOVE: Baker in the company whip.

When May and the crew arrived, we quickly learned what a circus is required to make a television show.

The sizzle had been shot with a skeleton crew, but the pilot was for real. We were green as a hayfield that's just been bailed, fumbling our way through a lot of it. We didn't know about "opening to the camera" (never talk with your back to the camera), being "camera unaware" (talk to the director, not into the lens), and not to wear white because it makes it too hard for the cameraman to balance the exposure. In order to account for our height differences—six feet six and five feet five—Erin had to stand on an apple box when we were in a shot together so we would look a little less like Beauty and the Beast.

It's strange, but I got used to the cameras

pretty quickly. A huge part of it is due to the team, who made it easy for us to be ourselves. The most awkward thing was the repetitive nature of filming, which was something we weren't prepared for. I knew that everything on television required multiple takes, but I guess I hadn't put much thought into how many times things have to be done. With only one camera—sometimes two—you have to repeat scenes over and over to get them from different angles. I took a theater class back in high school, but I'm no actor. Repeating scenes and making them feel as natural as the first time took some work.

The other issue I had was with messing up something on camera: making mistakes, getting ahead of myself, skipping steps, calling something by the wrong name, or measuring incorrectly. We've all been there, but doing it in front of a television camera? You're much more conscious of it. Everyone

LEFT: Me on my half-apple (half a full apple box) to make our heights more balanced in the frame.
TOP RIGHT: The one and only Lindsey Weidhorn.

is watching you, and you're taking up people's time, especially in a tight space or in the smothering Mississippi heat.

The pilot was set up just like the show is now: Erin and I get to know a couple, find out the kind of people they are and the kind of home they want. Then we hunt all over Laurel to narrow the possible homes down to two choices, while explaining our vision of what we would do to fix it up—salvaging and repurposing where we can, to hold on to the good and keep things under budget.

Those days of shooting were rough. We had to go through houses without air-conditioning in the sweltering heat explaining what we would do, trying to convince the homeowners that each house could fit the needs of their family. We had to communicate our vision of how we'd turn this run-down house into their forever home. Ross and Laura, the homeown-

ers in the pilot episode, had been friends of ours for a long time, which made it easier. And the Willett House, the one they bought, was one everyone in the neighborhood was excited to see transformed.

An aside here on the heat, which I can't ignore when discussing shooting this show: what makes the summers in Mississippi particularly miserable is the fact that you can't escape the humidity. Since we can't escape it, we try to distract ourselves from it. We swim in chlorinated pools that aren't much cooler than the air outside. Sometimes when we climb out of the pool, a breeze will blow and cool the water on your skin for a moment, if you're lucky. We call in orders of cherry Sprite to PDI, the oldest burger joint in town, because we know that if we wait until we get there to order, we'll be stuck sizzling outside in the parking lot while the cup fills up. We drink tall glasses of water or lemonade or tea in big, deep, shaded porches with a fan on us if we're lucky. These rituals may seem quaint, but they're really tactics of survival.

On that hot June day when Jim, Josh, and I went to Ross's family's cabin to salvage wood, we were all worried about one thing: snakes. Nobody had been down to that place in years. The overgrowth leading to the cabin was shoulder high, and there was a pond behind the cabin. In south Mississippi, that translates to one thing: water moccasins, venomous enough to kill you in a blink.

The cabin might've looked reparable on TV, but it wasn't: what you couldn't tell from watching the episode is that Hurricane Katrina had gotten the best of it ten years earlier and it was dangerously close to falling in. We probably shouldn't have been inside there at all.

But it was worth it. That cabin was part of Ross

ABOVE: The day before filming on the pilot began, we did a walk-through of the houses.

Behind the scenes filming the pilot.

More behind the scenes filming the pilot.

and Laura's history, so I used some of the wood for a giant dinner table I built for them as a gift. Now they can have family dinner on a table with a direct link to their past. I also used some of the cabin's wood for a kitchen island, along with a piece of the wall from the Willett House that became the base. It's important that the pieces I build tell a story—that's what makes them alive.

Using Laurel bricks in their fireplace hearth and getting black-and-white photos of their ancestors helped tie Ross and Laura's future to the family that had preceded them and the history of their new town. Everything about our style and approach—including saving what we could of the old and tying the present to the past—was already there in the pilot episode.

A few cool things didn't even make it into the episode, such as uncovering flooring boards that had been milled at Laurel's old Gilchrist sawmill, with the name stamped on the back; discovering a 1940s Coke bottle buried in a wall; and learning some more about the Willett House from Mrs. Hill, one of the neighbors. Mrs. Hill told us that when she was growing up her cousins had lived there, and they would put on plays and shows in the attic for the other kids in the neighborhood. Those details and stories bring a house together in a way that makes me feel the work is worthwhile. What Erin and I try to do is part of a large, continuous tale that binds us all together.

A pilot film crew is small and scrappy, with no assistants to move things in and out; those duties were left up to Erin and me, and so we brought in reinforcements—my little brother Jesse, Mallorie, Josh, and Jim—moving in our own furniture and blankets to make a corner feel finished, to make the rooms feel like a home, to fill out edges that needed filling.

The next day, dead tired, we had to move all the furnishings back where they'd come from. After wrapping, we spent an entire day on the couch, too wiped out to move. When we got hungry enough, we just about crawled into the kitchen to make some hot dogs for supper—anything else just wasn't going to happen.

Weeks later, after the circus left town, Erin and I found ourselves—in the dead of night—lighting candles and kneeling in prayer at the Episcopal church in our neighborhood. The sanctuary is left unlocked day and night for weary souls, for lighting candles, for prayer. There is something about kneeling at an altar and praying that makes it feel as though it counts a little more, even though it really doesn't. Maybe it just means more to us. Maybe that's the point.

On walks around the city late at night and into the early morning, Erin and I would talk about everything from children to business to the leaky faucet I needed to fix in our bathroom. Our feet became trained to walk to the big old wooden doors at St. John's and into the hushed silence, where it smelled warm and old, like furniture polish and birthday candles. While everyone else was sleeping, we would each light a candle before leaving all of our burdens on the altar. Prayers of hope, prayers of thanksgiving, prayers for wisdom, prayers of every kind.

I have a faith that something good will always happen. If the show had never gone forward, we would've continued doing exactly what we were doing, and we would have ended up exactly where we were supposed to be.

This was some BIG news for our little town.

17

A Show

Erin

Very early into filming season one of Home Town, *I realized that juggling Lucky Luxe and the show was going to be impossible.*

During a long walk one morning, I talked on the phone with a friend of mine who told me, "You have this garden with roses sprouting up, and you're grabbing at weeds to try and make a bouquet."

It was revelatory for me.

"I think it's time to trust that you've hit a fork in the road and it's okay to take it," she said.

A couple of months later, I sealed the last order of invitations and resolved to say good-bye to Lucky Luxe for a little while. It was bittersweet. But it was empowering, too.

In the meantime, Jim, Mallorie, Josh, and Emily convinced us that continuing erinandben.co could be fun and more manageable if we brought on partners. We all started dreaming bigger, imag-

ining a storefront in downtown Laurel, finally putting our money where our mouth was in our town by investing in a brick-and-mortar shop.

Josh had bought the dilapidated old Smith Furniture building on Front Street; he would renovate it, and we would reopen the Laurel Mercantile Co., which had closed in the 1930s. It would be a shop of American-made goods and heirloom wares, Ben's furniture, beautiful things for the home, tools, and Scotsman Co. workwear in a setting that was like stepping back into 1925. We believed that if we were going to be serious about small-town revitalization, it would have to start with supporting the American manufacturing that keeps small towns alive.

Photo by Lindsay Miller

Photo by Douglas Gautraud

Photo courtesy of The Market Beautiful

TOP LEFT: The framily and the Mercantile, before. | TOP RIGHT: The framily and the Mercantile on opening day!
BOTTOM: Inside our little shop of American-made heirloom wares and durable goods.

After three seasons we've found our rhythm making *Home Town*, but that doesn't mean it's easy or automatic. For six months of the year our lives revolve around filming. If either Ben or I has to take a day off, it messes up everyone's schedule and complicates everyone else's job. So we don't. The whole production is a whirlwind, intense and demanding, and it takes a lot of talented people and tons of work for it not to look that way onscreen.

We've all become a little family and have found a way to make it work, to keep it lively and fun, and, most important, to keep the spirit of its purpose: shining a light on our little town and maybe even inspiring others to do the same for their own.

The reality of it involves a bleary 4:45 a.m. wake-up. In the dark, Ben heads to the gym and I go for a long walk around the neighborhood with our dogs and my headphones—Journey and José González pushing me up hills and into the sunrise, with my heartbeat thrumming while I'm reminded to keep believing, to step outside and leave it all behind me. The exercise helps wake us up and also helps us look awake: it ensures that our faces aren't puffy when the cameras begin rolling at 7 a.m. We make it back home just as the sun is rising and the cicadas begin to sing the song of Mississippi. Over coffee, cereal, and eggs, we chat—usually about what needs to get done before sundown.

"Jonathan's free to reshoot the scene with the porch ceiling leak," I'll say, "so I packed you two navy blue shirts."

"Got it," Ben will say, distracted as he reads the news on his phone.

"Don't sweat too hard if you can help it. Two will have to last you all day."

"I'll do my best," Ben will say. "Remind me I gotta change the oil in the truck."

"It'll have to wait till Saturday," I'll tell him, "when we're not shooting.

"What do you need to finish the piano desk for the Holloways?" I'll ask.

"I don't think I'll finish it in time. It's gonna kill me first." (But of course he'll finish, at 2 a.m. the night before the reveal.)

When filming, we work on three or four houses at a time, called blocks. With Ben's thermos of iced coffee and my stuffed set bag we hop into the old Scotsman truck. Even if the house is down the street, we always drive because of the clown car amount of tools and lumber and clothes and rugs and lamps that travel with us.

We begin at house number one while the sun is not yet hot enough to roast us. Tim Harland, our director of photography since the pilot, is already there: cargo pants, a bandanna around his curly salt-and-pepper hair, the round glasses of a college professor. He greets us with a jovial "Good MORNING! Sweaty hugs!"

Tim has a way of making every person he talks to feel interesting and important, loved and celebrated. He always brings everyone back snacks from his faraway travels and hosts regular chili suppers for the whole cast and crew. Tim has also embraced his temporary home

ABOVE: Tim Harland, everyone's favorite DP. His middle name is Pride, and we found that sign in the old grocery near my parents' house.

in a way that embodies the way our crew has embedded themselves into the community. One season he got stuck living in an apartment complex for the elderly (we don't have many apartment options in town), but he never complained. When an ailing neighbor, who had no family, was in the hospital, he went to visit her every evening after we wrapped. That's the kind of person he is.

The rest of the camera team is always close by, setting up along with Jim, our director seasons one and three, in his trademark shorts and tan. Young and full of silly energy, he always looks as though

he just came out of the surf to eat tacos on Venice Beach. He's a Canadian turned Californian having a love affair with Mississippi. After greeting us with hugs, he sends us inside to get "mic'd up."

Three years in, the microphone packs on our waistbands and boots for twelve hours a day feel like part of our own anatomy. Ben and I find ourselves editing conversations even when we're completely alone in the car or our kitchen, always unsure if our voices are being recorded.

My favorite scenes to film are the on-the-fly interviews (OTFs), where it's just me (standing on my box), Ben, Tim with the camera, Joel with the lights, and Jim, who asks us questions about the scene we just filmed. These are always done in a park or off to the side of the construction. Our directors know how to coax a good story or joke out of us, always asking the question that evokes the most interesting answer possible: a silly song and dance we made up while checking in on the new floors, the unplanned moments of chatter between Ben and me.

One day we were in Daphne Park waiting for the train to pass through town so we could shoot an OTF. A few nights earlier, I had been snacking on some candied almonds that Drew and Jonathan Scott (the Property Brothers) had sent us as a thank-you for doing a guest appearance on their show. While chewing I had felt a painful crunch that had me chewing on the other side of my mouth all day. That afternoon in the park, waiting for the train to pass, Ben and I were sitting in the crook of a low-growing oak tree branch. I was chewing gum when I felt part of my tooth break off into it—and full panic ensued. Filming stopped so I could run to the dentist, who repaired a piece of a filling that had broken off. I returned to finish the interview, numb mouth and all.

Between scenes we always end up wandering by craft services, the show business term for "where the snacks are." Ben and I are always sneak-

ABOVE: Loblollipops after lunch is an on-set treat.

TOP LEFT: An OTF during the Warren episode, season one. | TOP RIGHT: First day of filming season one. | BOTTOM LEFT: You never know what surprises we leave under the paint in these houses. | BOTTOM RIGHT: The Men of Mercantile.

TOP: I designed T-shirts for the cast and crew for what felt like summer camp to all of us.
BOTTOM LEFT: Wardrobe photos are taken before every scene so if we do a reshoot, we can replicate the look.
BOTTOM RIGHT: Tim and Big catnapping on lunch break.

ing handfuls of peanut butter pretzels. Later I'll be eating pickles while waiting for the tile guy to arrive to film our scene. I'll sit on the grass and watch Ben drink coffee with one hand, throwing a football with Joel, one of our camera operators.

If there's a delay, we nap in the car for a few minutes and get our second wind before climbing under a house or taking out cabinetry. Some days we run a gauntlet of tasks, and a race against the clock to finish before we lose the daylight and filming has to shut down.

If we're waiting around for plumbers or roofing people to arrive, the football comes back out and the guys play in the yard while I sit in a bag chair wondering how long it'll take someone to turn an ankle or knee. I usually sit with Tim, who is smart enough to know the value of his ankles and his knees.

Lunch in the production office is usually Mexican food or some kind of baked chicken with roasted potatoes around a big table where cast and crew eat together like a family. We're always famished enough to eat two plates, relishing an hour in the air-conditioning. Then it's out the door, grabbing a shortbread cookie on our way

to the truck and house number two, then number three, then number four before the sun goes down.

Toward the end of construction is when I get to decorate the house. I first go to our clients' current home and take anything that works with my idea, with their style or story: books, photos, art, furnishings, flags, whatever I find that strikes my fancy. Then it's time to shop. I almost always take Mallorie along because it's like a competitive sport to her; she will see something I completely miss and then she will haggle for it until she gets it for the best price. We have the same taste, so she knows my heart and mind. If I'm zeroed in on finding a chair, she will notice an antique crock for flowers on the front porch that is just perfect.

Other shops all over Laurel and south Mississippi will kindly loan us the remaining pieces we need. Some pieces of furniture are part of the design budget, and everything Ben builds for the new homeowners is a gift. The days go on like this, every day much the same but different in that we never know what will spring up in each house: what new discovery, delay, or dilemma awaits. That's part of the experience.

Being involved in a television series never feels like anything more than making a short film promoting our little town, just as we used to do all the time for the local news or with our talented friend, the local cinematographer Brandon Davis. It feels like since we're a part of

TOP: The guys on set said the cotton candy grapes tasted like regular old grapes and I was just a sucker for marketing.
BOTTOM: Big and Brandon. We miss him every day.

ABOVE and OPPOSITE: More behind the scenes.

Photo by Timothy P. Harland, Artison Productions LLC.

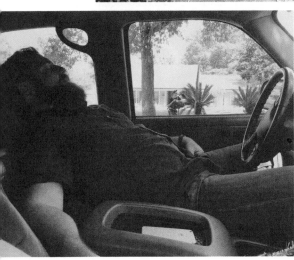

More behind the scenes of *Home Town*.

Completing shot!

This does not seem real —

Last day of Season 2

Filming the last scene of season two in the Trests' backyard.

it, it simply isn't a big deal. It's normalized a pretty abnormal thing, simply by seeing ourselves attached to it. No matter how long we do it, I know that we'll never let it feel any different.

Ben

In all the important ways, *Home Town* is really just an extension of the lives Erin and I were already living: the way we went about renovating our loft and then our house, making the most of our unique skills, being inventive where we didn't have the money, looking to the past to make sure the homes told a story.

The show made sense as part of the overall mission. With each house we saved, we felt we were putting Laurel back on its rightful place on the map.

These houses are places of history, love, and beauty that have been neglected and forgotten. We work to connect the house with the next people who will spend their lives there, whose story will unfold under its roof.

Of course, all that sentimental good stuff begins with the first step: taking things apart. Demo looks fun, and it is—I get to tap into my inner child. Since I was a kid, I've always loved taking things apart. Part of my motivation was to learn how they were made, but the real thrill for me was making things better. When I would assemble model car kits, I wanted to change little details. Most of the time, I'd get the car apart and couldn't for the life of me get it back together.

The show was also an expansion of what was already happening in downtown Laurel, which had been going through a revitalization—celebrating its history while focusing on the future.

Erin and I tackle houses according to the same precepts of the journal that she religiously kept every single day for eight years: recognizing the beauty in what is already there, dreaming big, using our imagination to bring something to life, and connecting with the things that warm our hearts.

When you watch *Home Town*, the demo sometimes looks as though we are just smashing things, but the reality is that we're pretty careful. I prefer to peel back the layers of a house slowly. If we carefully remove the countertops in a kitchen, we might be able to save the cabinets. If we pry off paneling or sheetrock, we might discover beadboard or some other tongue-grooved wood. We're essentially digging for treasure. That's not to say I don't enjoy smashing something once in a while, because who doesn't?

The whole process is one of discovery—or rediscovery. Laurel was founded as a lumber town, and all that yellow pine went into floors in our historic district's homes. Very often we pull up carpet or tile to find the wood hiding underneath, just waiting for someone—usually Mike, our hardwood specialist—to find it again.

Every house in Laurel is named for the family who built it or who lived in it the longest. That's because the story of a house is the story of people's lives, just as Mrs. Mary Lynn's and Laurel's first dentist's and Lauren Rogers's story are all intimately tied to the story of our home. It's the identity of the house—part of its bones and blood—and we want to make sure that's not ignored or erased.

I think of our job as adding to its story. Erin hunts through antiques stores to find objects that

make sense in the new home. She is adamant about not buying things just because they're aesthetically pleasing. It's a question of connection: What does this mean to the homeowners? What could it mean? I ask the same question when I build a piece of furniture, especially if I use reclaimed materials that have some personal connection to the home buyers.

Sometimes we'll tie a house back to its own history, like when we dressed a room of an old World War II boardinghouse by bringing in a framed red cross, old maps, pictures, and local newspapers to put up on the walls. Other times we're injecting the homeowner's history into the new house, for example, by using the wrought iron from a family's old home for a bench's end caps or its wood to build a new dining room table. Once in a while it's a ridiculous idea we've never tried, like when we literally picked up and moved Robyn's great-grandmother's house to new land in season two.

For every home we've done for the show we try to work in as many elements as possible of the philosophy that anchors our work:

Knowing the people: Before we do anything, Erin and I sit down and have a long talk with the homeowners. We also ask them to fill out a survey that asks both obvious questions and not-so-obvious ones: What is their most treasured "weird" item, what are their favorite books and music and childhood memories. This part is for both sides of the transaction: On their end, they're building trust in us, which is key since they're turning their home (and, by extension, their future) over to us. On our end, we can't design a home without having a good grasp of people's hopes, personality, and vision.

For the Smith House, we learned about Aly's

love for the 1920s and 1930s and the literature from that era, her and Jordan's taste for neutral colors and comfortable leather sofas, but Erin is great at going deeper than people's favorite colors and styles and getting into their identity and dreams and turning that into a kind of a template. She's imagining their mind-set with each choice she makes. It's an impressive ability.

Knowing the house: This has to do with accepting what the house is and isn't, what it can and can't be. You can't just superimpose your wishes on top of a house without considering the base point you're starting with. It's like people: how I wasn't built for a life in the ministry and Erin wasn't built for a life in the corporate world. The house already has an

ABOVE: Aly and Jordan's house was a favorite of season two.

identity, and we work to accentuate that in line with the home buyers' wishes. The Ratcliff House was a mishmash of various identities, so one of our jobs was to choose a direction for it.

From the outside, the Ratcliff House looked unbalanced, with more windows on one side than the other. Instead of hiding this, which was nearly impossible, Erin and I decided to play it up by removing the screens from one side of the porch to make the imbalance look intentional.

Inside, beneath the plaster, we found a patchwork of rough-hewn cabin wood that wouldn't make sense for the formal house Caroline envisioned. We sheetrocked over it, though we kept a plank that we found from the house's birth, dated in blue chalk: Jan 2, 1906— Laurel, Miss. We framed it and placed it on the wall in the dining room, right in front of the spot where we'd found it. It was just too perfect.

Understanding what a house is involves removing the layers of time to discover both the good (hardwood under-der flooring or a fireplace behind a wall) and the bad (bats or rotted wood). All are part of what the home is. Our job is to embrace the good and find a way to work forward from there.

Telling a story: Each house tells a story, but it also is a story in itself. As a person walks through a house, it unfolds, almost like a narrative. The entrance is the thing that gets your attention and lures you in, and we try to play it up. There is a foreshadowing, a hint of what's to come, in the first room of any house you enter. There's suspense, as when something hidden is revealed. There are small moments that add up to a powerful payoff.

In the Ponder House, things unfolded like this: The front porch was a retreat for Luke, a bachelor and outdoorsman who wanted a place to sit outside and listen to baseball on the radio. The porch felt like a man's place—minimal, comfortable, a hall tree near

the door with ball caps and a jacket hanging close at hand. Then the living room unfolded, revealing a little more about that kind of person he is: fly-fishing rods on the wall, oil paintings of the great wide open, oak limbs cut that morning instead of fresh flowers on the coffee table. Leather, books, and tartan.

Those things gave way to his study, where there was a massive wall of his books and collections: vinyl records, antique baseballs, cigar boxes. The house actually looked like him, each room revealing more about him as you walked through it, just like reading

ABOVE: The Ponder House living room and study.

a book, developing the protagonists, the homeowners, as you go along. Each room was a "chapter in the book of the house," as Erin likes to say.

Rediscovering and reusing: When we pulled up the carpet in Cory and Caroline's future office, we found cognac-colored hardwood that had been hidden for decades. The final home office ended up looking completely different from the pink room we had first encountered. But so much of the bones of what it became—the wainscoting, the fireplace, the beams, and the floors—was already there.

When we removed the upper kitchen cabinets, I took the oak from them and made an end-grain butcher block. We removed a section of beadboard from one of the walls and made it into a coffee table, had old bricks from the fireplace sliced up and turned those into the kitchen backsplash. We also

found an old brick chimney behind one of the living room walls that we ended up leaving exposed. All those elements originated with the house itself. What we do is make choices that add up to a home that feels purposeful, well thought out, and unified.

Whether it's turning porch windows into cabinets or an old screen door into a pantry door, I'm interested in the idea of rebirth. It's about uniting past and future, recognizing that we don't always want to get rid of things, that a new purpose can breathe new life into them. It's embracing the circle of life.

Being resourceful: This is about making do with what you have and creating what you can't afford. It's Erin finding a French Provençal basket at the flea market and turning it upside down to make a chandelier in the Carson House or me taking an old upright piano in the living room and transforming it

into a desk for the Holloways. For the Tews' home in the pilot episode, Erin wanted linen curtains in the living room and office, which were too expensive for our design budget. She thought about what would have the same coloring and texture as linen but would be more affordable: hardware store canvas drop cloths. She and her mom made curtains for the whole house in one afternoon for a couple hundred dollars. Some version of this always comes up because it's our natural inclination to be creative when we come up against a challenge, budgetary or otherwise.

Seeing past the surface/visualizing the future: In just about every episode, even the savviest home buyer gets thrown off by an ugly wall color, dated wallpaper, or some fad that has not aged well. But those are the easiest things to change. This is such a common reaction that it reminds me how much we're all affected by the surface of things, when we shouldn't be. It's why people bury treasure.

On day one of the renovation we often tear that surface off and find something underneath that is not just worth salvaging but perfectly in line with what makes sense for the house. It reminds us not to be fooled by first appearances and that craftsmanship lasts long after trends have faded.

Creating teamwork and community: Erin and I are constantly playing off each other, working in tandem, bringing each other's vision to life. Of course, we also lean on the local community, letting the experts—landscapers, electricians, and others—do their thing. It's why for the pilot episode we invited all the people who had helped us restore the house, who were also their neighbors, to greet Ross and Laura on the porch at the end of the show. It wasn't just good television; it sent a very real message that we believe in: this couple is not just buying a home; they're entering a community and beginning a new life. The house is just the first step of their journey.

ABOVE: The team that made season two possible.

The day we announced publicly that our family was growing. *Photo by Brooke Davis*

18

A Future

Erin

Years ago, in 2011, Ben's younger brother Tom and his wife, Allison, welcomed a baby girl into the world.

When we got to the hospital, I watched Tom, taller than Ben and just as sturdy, hold tiny sleeping Harper against his body. I remember softening toward my brother-in-law with the hard exterior, considering the life and blood he shared with my husband, whom I know better almost than myself. And in that moment I could almost picture Ben just like that: with our newborn sleeping on his chest.

About a month later, we got the news that my brother, Clark, and his wife, Amanda, had begun the process of adopting a child. Around Christmas, Mallorie and Jim met us at Cotton Blues for corn bread, shrimp, and grits and told us that they, too, were going to be having a baby. Mallorie and I began quietly crying there at the table. She and I had always talked about one day having children at the same time who would grow up together. It had long been hypothetical, but when that day became real for her, I felt a new tenderness toward her but a sadness as well. She was going before me, and I was being left behind.

That Christmas, visiting Ben's parents, I spent an afternoon coloring Ben's mom's hair and painting her nails. She has lived a long girlless existence with all those men in the house. Ben was nearby, sorting through old family photos, and came across one of Tom, Ben's dad (whom we call The Rev), and Ben. He handed it to me, and it stopped me cold.

That face.

ABOVE: The photo I found that day at Ben's parents' house.

I could not stop staring at that round face under a mop of dark blond hair. It was the face of what my little boy would look like. It communicated the reality of children to my heart in a way that had never happened before. I saw a boy who would be brave and kind and loving and tough. Who would get stains on his shirt and runny noses and skinned knees. My heart seized up at how much I would love him.

It made sense that an old photo would trigger that reaction, because it's how we'd always done things: houses, invitations, journal entries. By looking back to that frozen moment of time, I was able to look forward, imagine a future that I had the power to create.

I was in my late twenties at the time, and the prospect of being a mother still seemed too big for me. For years I had long felt a heartache that I could not name, caused by a fear that I could not shake. But as children came into the lives of our family and friends, something inside me opened up. I became less afraid. I knew that one day I would have just an ounce more courage than I had the day before.

Our mothers had been afraid, too, though we hadn't known it. They'd made sure of that; we only remember being loved. We recall the Friday-afternoon visits to Cotton Mill Park, where we ate McDonald's french fries on the picnic tables, the bubble baths where we would use our fingers to write letters in foamy white soap on their backs. And then they were afraid again, when we set out on our own and all they could do was hope. We believed that they knew nothing when they knew everything and that they should have trusted us more, though they were right not to.

Ben and I had often wondered what the secret was, how to raise children to become good people, loving souls, happy adults. When Ben worked in youth ministry, we saw so many kids grow up and move on. We were always wondering, as we said good-bye, if there was something we could have done to set them on the right path. It led me to want to know more about what my parents had done when raising us.

So I asked them. And Daddy gave me a list:

1. Let your children know that even though you love them the most, they are no better than anyone else.

2. Make sure they understand love means showing discipline, which you have to do every time they do something they shouldn't. Every time.

3. Do what you can to keep them focused on the right things, the ones that matter: being thoughtful, being prepared, and being kind.

4. Spend all the time you can with them, especially when they're little.

As I turned thirty and my parents turned sixty, I went through what we all do: thoughts on life, death, and who will care when I'm gone. I wondered what my life would mean if there was no one, no son or daughter, to care that it happened, to carry on the precious traditions and stories our parents gave us. Someday, we will be only the stories we leave behind to the people who care enough to share them.

And when those thoughts find their way in, as they often do, and I get scared or overwhelmed, I have a good cry. Then I take a long walk and have a talk with God, even when I'm too upset to make sense. I speak to my best friends until I realize something I never would have thought of; then I take a long bath, watch an old episode of *Felicity*, and let Big tell me, "We will figure it all out tomorrow," while I lie with my head on his solid chest. And I trust that we will.

But some things felt harder to get my arms around.

Motherhood had long been my greatest fear—and a shameful one at that. As a six-year-old I had seen childbirth photos in Daddy's medical textbook and had never been able to shake the images. But I didn't want to be afraid of it. I wanted to be like the other women in my life—and everywhere else—who never considered pregnancy something to be feared. I wanted so badly to be brave.

Every single night, when I turned out the bedside light, I asked myself, "Will I ever be brave enough? For all of it?"

I read recently that when you let routine take over your life, your brain goes into autopilot and stops recording, almost as though it knows: Nothing to see here. Nothing new, nothing worth remembering. You have to do and see new things for your brain to take snapshots that make life feel lasting. As much as trying new things scared me, I resolved to start. And hoped that it would get easier.

After going to bed at eight o'clock the night before, I woke up on Mother's Day 2017 feeling that something was off. I was more tired than I had ever been; my body was heavy like

My Thirtieth Birthday

When I woke up on August 1, Ben worked his magic once again with a little book he had made called "30 Days of Erin." I had been struggling with waves of sadness and worry as my thirtieth birthday approached and I was still childless, though beginning to feel the pangs of bravery that made me think I'd someday be ready. At the time, my biological clock was louder than anything else in my life, and it was deafening. As I read this book he had made me, I started to cry. I had thirty days left to be a twenty-something, thirty days to celebrate being alive and turning thirty.

He had planned an entire month of activities and trips to celebrate all the things I loved most from childhood all the way through my twenties in an effort to teach me that even though we get older we are the same people. The things we loved as kids can be the things we love as adults, and each day

he challenged me to prove it to myself: go swimming with my mom at Lake Waukaway, take a late-night trip to New Orleans for karaoke on Bourbon Street, eat my favorite meal, go to a concert. He even planned out three entirely different road trips, made a book of the options, and left it up to me to choose which one we would take, which ended up being Austin, Texas, to see Damien Rice perform for the first time ever so we got to hear the soundtrack of our falling in love in real time in a theater.

The month ended with a last-minute trip to New York City, and I rang in my thirtieth birthday at midnight with Lindsey, our HGTV executive, and her friends in a beach house on the shore. I had found my zeal for the next leg of the journey and whatever it would bring thanks to Big.

lead, slow like molasses. And I just knew. I weakly made it to the bathroom to take a test, which confirmed it. Another unplanned moment was about to change our life.

"What does this mean?" I asked the groggy Ben, holding out the small stick with the pink lines. "What does this mean?" I kept asking for lack of anything else to say.

But he knew. The news brought him to life, and as he wrapped his big arms around me, he said, "It's great. Everything is going to be great." Before lunch, he was already drawing up designs for the crib.

It would be the scariest and most important thing we would ever do, and each morning when I opened my eyes and remembered, it washed over me: the feeling of relief, that we were finally brave enough. The fear hadn't gone away. It was just that our hopes and our love had outweighed it. We knew we were headed to a new normal come January. I was afraid of all that would come, but I knew it would teach us to stretch and grow and learn things we never could have otherwise. I knew we'd be grateful for it, because we will know we are making something good.

If we had been the great planners we thought we were, Ben might have become a history professor or a lawyer and I might be working for a magazine—two amazing careers, both of which would be astoundingly wrong for us. We have learned that the places to which He leads us usually have nothing to do with what we think will make us happy.

Happiness comes through giving to others, which incidentally brings it back to you tenfold. We've learned firsthand that if you want to walk on water, you have to get out of the boat. I pray for the hearts of the people we love who are in an endless struggle to find their joy in life. It never ends for any of us, and I pray we can all keep looking for the cues.

That fall, on the set of *Home Town*, I sat in Ben's truck at a construction site, laptop open on my swollen belly, banished outside because of the fumes from the oil paint. As I wrote that day's

journal, I was thinking about how we do not control our future; we are only participants. If we're willing to give in to where God leads us, scary though it may be, we'll keep landing in the right place.

Ben was inside building tapered columns in a living room, and I could see all of it: young children one day climbing those columns, imagining they are pirates and the columns are their ships, leaving chocolate fingerprints on the varnish.

At home, our own transformation was slowly unfolding. The guest room was becoming our daughter's room, so we emptied out the sparse furnishings that have moved with us since college: the metal bed that belonged to my grandparents, the pine desk from my apartment at Ole Miss, the little hope chest Ben made for me on our second Christmas. Our daughter's childhood will unfold in a room that once held the stories from our past. It's perfect.

Ben

Within an hour of Erin telling me that we were going to have a baby, after the tears but before the phone calls, I set about working on the crib. I was at the computer looking up safety regulations and dimensions for baby cribs while Erin yelled to me from the other room, "Ben, that can wait!" I knew it could, but it would be the most special piece I'd ever had the opportunity to build. And I wanted to get started.

But I already knew what I wanted: white oak. The crib would become something far beyond furniture: I would use it to teach our child about what it is that I do. There'd be beautiful figure in the wood, fine joinery, and it would perfectly match our home. The craftsmanship would have to be something

ABOVE: May 14, 2017, for the first time, I accepted the rose given to all women on Mother's Day during church and felt a secret joy I'd never had before.

Ben building the baby crib.

special, representing the weight and import of who would sleep there. I saved one piece of old-growth heart pine from our house to fill a knothole in one of the top rails, and I took care to cut the board so it landed dead center. Her first bed would forever have a piece of her first home, as it should be.

For the back panel, I ordered a sheet of quarter-sawn white oak veneer. It was the most expensive piece of wood I'd ever worked with and the first time I'd ever worked with a veneer—so no pressure. Then I used my shaper table to create some custom trim. I shaped the edges of two white oak boards and then stacked them, which gave the effect of a crown on the back panel. I also made some smooth, rounded pieces for the top rail on three sides, imagining our baby someday pulling up and using the rail for a teething toy.

Erin loves spooled legs on furniture, a wood-turning style that gives the look of vertically stacked balls. I found a way to have two spools at the bottom and one on the top. I thinned down some golden oak stain, already a light color, which gave just enough color to make the grain stand out without hiding the natural beauty of the wood. I jointed the four panels with pocket-hole screws so we could convert the bed to a toddler bed and then to a twin bed: it'll last longer if it can transform as our child does.

Erin

We painted the nursery's walls and brought in the heirloom crib Ben had built, which brought me to pieces when I finally saw it there in her room. I brought in the sconces that remind me of our favorite old inn in Massachusetts, the antique pine dresser from Europe that will become her changing table, the threadbare Persian rug in coral and greens and blues that she'll learn to crawl on. I could picture myself in the blue linen wingback

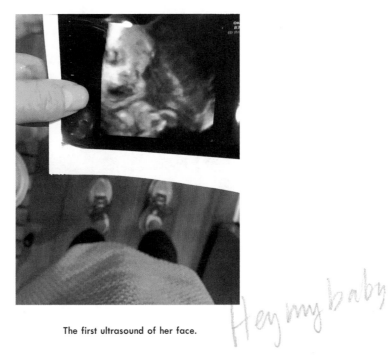

The first ultrasound of her face.

Hey my baby

Three days before Helen

rocker, cradling her on a sleepless night, quieting her cries by singing "God Will Take Care of You."

Until she arrived, I relished our quiet nights at home. Just Ben and me, animals burrowing together for the winter, arms looped through each other's as we read at bedtime. Just the two of us, the way it had always been. The way it wouldn't always be.

He ran me baths, made me grilled cheese sandwiches, and before bed he pulled the covers over his head, moved down beside my belly, and spoke so low I couldn't hear, talking to our unborn child. It took the longest time to tell people; I just had a gut feeling something would go wrong. And I didn't want to let myself get my hopes up about her. I let go of that feeling only when the doctor assured me, "If she were born today, she would be viable." But I still carried some fear.

Fear about going through it at all: the cold air of the hospital, the beeps of machines, the gleaming silver tools, the blood.

Fear of how the sound of her cry would break some unused spaces of my heart wide open.

Fear that I would be wholly responsible for feeding her with nothing but my body, designed to do that very specific thing from the moment of my own birth. I wondered whether I would completely lose myself or finally recognize myself.

Even with Ben there every step of the way, the bond between my daughter and me is where it all began; her ability to survive and grow is all mine.

But then I felt it: there is power in remembering the good that has already come to us. We all got here somehow, in our own way, not according to our parents' plans. And we're still here. And we will go on, as we were meant to do, continuing to make something good each day.

OPPOSITE: Helen's nursery, which was not finished until many weeks after she was born.
ABOVE: New Year's Eve 2018, three days before the baby came.

I tried to snap Polaroids of her the day we came home from the hospital.
This one made me laugh, then cry. Our tiny Super Bunny, swallowed up by a newborn-size romper, floating off into the sky.

Epilogue

Erin

She surprises us by coming almost three weeks early. Her crib isn't finished. Her nursery isn't done. We are not ready, though I know we will never be ready.

She is healthy but tiny, not quite six pounds. Her hair strawberry blond, her eyes pools of blue, her fingers long and thin. Her cry is not the tinny and screeching one I'd imagined but soft, like a lamb's. When I hold her warm face to my chest, it fills my heart to overflowing. It's almost too much to bear. I'd waited for her for so long. She was an idea, and now she is a person.

We name her Helen, for my grandmother, whom we called Meemaw, who looked like a 1960s movie star, who snapped aloe plants on burned fingers, who kept a secret stash of orange marshmallow circus peanuts in a cookie jar, who had a heart-shaped face, which our baby inherits.

Ben has a plastered-on smile for days, like a child getting to celebrate an early Christmas. We bring her home on a Saturday morning in January, Ben making a playlist for the car ride that makes us both cry, then filming every step as we first enter the house. As though for the first time, because our life is beginning anew.

When we first lay Helen in her crib, Ben gets teary-eyed and doesn't rub the tears away. He brings me close as we stare: How in the world can we improve on this?

Once she falls asleep, I allow myself to feel this new reality. More weary than I ever thought possible, I take a long shower. The hot water will leave my skin red and splotchy. Everything has changed, I think. I am a mother now. I touch the thick black incision across my belly and feel grateful: my biggest fear is now forever behind me.

For four weeks, we lock ourselves in at home. When she sleeps, we try to sleep too, in two-hour blocks. When we can't, we stare like zombies at the TV: *Tommy Boy, Braveheart, Forrest Gump, The Big Lebowski.*

Some mornings without having had enough sleep to be able to think straight, I hold Helen close to me and wonder if our life will ever be normal again. I cry over the littlest thing and for no reason at all, several times a day. Underneath, I know I'm just tired in the most unnatural way. It is a new feeling. The sleeplessness of the first few weeks and a strict no-visitors policy to avoid the flu epidemic bring on an aching loneliness. I miss our friends more than I thought possible.

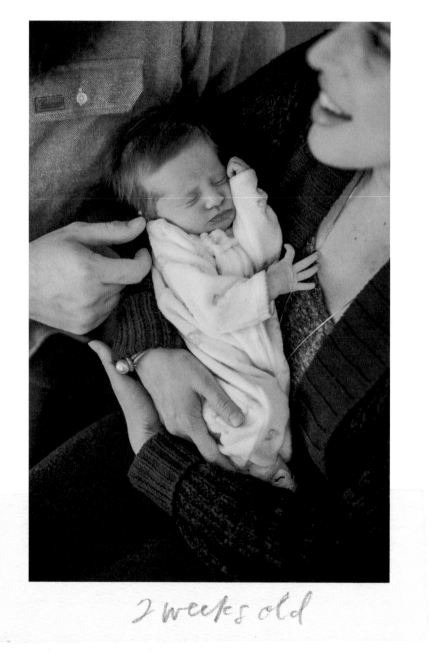

2 weeks old

Photo by Brooke Davis

"It'll get easier," Ben's dad tells me on the phone. "She's just figuring you out, and you're figuring her out."

We struggle to find our footing, to comprehend her language, understand what she needs from her cries and coos. It's always hunger or tiredness. Ben gets excited when he thinks he's figured out which is which.

"Hungry crying gets louder and more intense the more she waits for a bottle," he says. "Like we are not going to feed her."

"Uh-huh," I say.

"And then there's tired crying," he continues. "Tired crying is whiny. She cries for a few seconds, then forgets all about it. Then she cries a little more and then gets distracted by the ceiling fan . . ."

I am too tired to hear him out, but he sounds as though he is onto something.

Ben is amazing, remembering to whisper when Helen naps, while I always fall back into my normal volume. He lets me sleep when he can, sitting up with Helen and holding her while she cries when we can't think of anything else to do. One morning I find him filing her paper-thin baby nails. Another morning she's in her swing, beaming, Ben drinking a cup of coffee beside her, a book open on his lap. He is particularly excited by how much she already loves being read to. She follows the pages and lights up as if she were actually reading already. He thinks she might be.

By week six, Helen surprises us. I hear crying, but when I open my eyes, the sunshine is peeking through the cracks behind the shades. Once we can finally sleep through the night more than once, our old selves return along with warmer days.

When we stand over her crib in the new morning, she smiles, laughs, and kicks, and it makes my heart feel all of it—the sun rising, the birds singing, our little miracle coming to life. I search her face for what has changed overnight. It's subtle, but it's there: a furrowed brow like my grandfather's, a grin like our niece Ellie's. She knows Ben's voice and looks for him when she hears it. We both know it's because of those nights he spoke to her under the cover, through my belly. A message from her future.

We want her childhood to be as normal as possible, without the pressure of a camera that might warp the heart and mind that are growing inside her. I worry about being away from her when she's little, wanting to be with her the way our mothers were there with us. I know we'll never be far away when filming begins again, but my heart aches at the thought of nine hours without her each day. When the worry gets to be too much, I push it out of my mind to focus on the present: the coos, the diapers, the bottles, the songs I make up in the bath with her, the way she will lie on Ben's chest for hours if he lets her.

On our quiet walks around the neighborhood each afternoon, she is alert, anxious to see this strange new world. I point out the cars passing by, the dogs barking, the houses that dot our streets. I think of one day holding her hand as we walk back from the bakery, taking the long way home so she can point out her favorite house to me again.

When Helen is three months old, Ben tells me he already is missing those early days. That sweet, skinny baby with the big eyes, the wrinkled fore-

One month. Two months. Three months.

head, the pensive look of staring out the window as the wind shakes the oak branches. When Ben goes back to the wood shop, he says he's afraid Helen will look different when he comes home or that she will learn how to roll over and he will miss it. But he doesn't miss a thing.

I dreamed of Helen before she was born and saw a chubby baby with wrinkles at her wrists and thighs, a moony smile on her face. All I could think about was meeting her, hoping and praying she would love me the way I love my own mama.

Now I find myself searching her face for the teenager she'll become, wondering who she will be, where she will go, what she will do.

I want her to love to read, to lose herself in books about faraway people and places.

I want her to see the magic in climbing trees, the closest we can get to flying like birds.

I want to teach her how to make my mom's lasagna and Ben's mom's blue velvet cake.

I want her to love old cars and the satisfaction that comes with working for yourself and feeling spent down to your bones at the end of the day.

I want to see Ben wade out into the ocean with her on his hip, for her to splash in the waves and pretend she is a mermaid.

I want her to marry a good man who loves her well, the way Ben loves us. It feels too far away to be real, but I know it's only a few sleeps away. Life works like that. The waiting takes years. Then it comes all at once.

We are starting over once more, opening our arms and eyes and hearts to this strange world that is emerging through our daughter's eyes. And we will see it, too. All over again, I want to share this way of seeing, where everything is possible and new and good, and I never want to look away.

Sweet baby Helen.

Author's Note

Erin

In college, I was the design editor of our award-winning yearbook. In art school, I did a series of Ernest Hemingway book jackets as a semester-long project. Type, photos, and illustration were my favorite mediums, and my plan was to be a graphic designer in the publishing industry when I graduated, designing magazines or books until I retired. As you've learned, my plans didn't happen the way I had imagined, but it has been a joy to design the cover and pages of this book we dreamed of for so long.

I arranged a collection of objects from our life together and took the back cover photo to always remember those days and seasons I documented for so many years:

QUARTER-SAWN WHITE OAK
Ben used to build Helen's crib
BEN'S FAVORITE RED BROOKLYN HAT
worn throughout the campaign and in the wood shop when he's on a deadline
DRIED GINKGO LEAVES
from the tree beside our first apartment, showered over us after our wedding
BEN'S SUNDAY WATCH
always worn with his suits and ties
A LETTERPRESS AIRMAIL ENVELOPE
from my wedding stationery company, Lucky Luxe
MY FAVORITE JAPANESE WATERCOLOR PALETTE
used for every house portrait on Home Town
THE HANDKERCHIEF SAVE-THE-DATE
that put Lucky Luxe in the international spotlight
MY EYEGLASSES
necessary when I don't have contacts since I'm nearly blind
THE SEVENTH ANNIVERSARY BOOK
handmade by Ben just like the six before it
OUR WEDDING RINGS

Acknowledgments

To our parents, thank you for loving us, but mostly for loving each other. You show us what deep, abiding love and commitment look like, and we are lucky to have your example.

To our brothers, Clark, Sam, Tom, and Jesse, our protectors and friends who know all the secrets that exist in the blank spaces of these stories.

To our framily, Jim, Mallorie, Josh, and Emily, our partners and confidantes: without you, the ideas might vanish, doing our job would be impossible, and our world would be very lonely.

To Aunt Phyllis, Aunt Mae, Kelsa, and Steve: aunts and cousins are backup mamas and siblings, and your influence looms large in ways you can't imagine.

To Jennifer Bergstrom, Lauren McKenna, Marla Daniels, Jaime Putorti, Lisa Litwack, and the rest of our team at Simon & Schuster, thank you for giving us the creative freedom to make this the book we wanted so badly.

To Jon Sternfeld, thank you for taking our words and shining them up, for making us dig deeper when we thought we'd said enough.

To our literary agent, Kim Perel, thank you for being our advocate and for your superpower ability to summarize the breadth and depth of an entire life in the fewest words possible.

To Kit, Jenna, Toni, Lerner, Allison, Santos, Abbi, Kathleen, and the rest of our RTR Media and HGTV families, thank you for the most unexpected chapter imaginable in the book of our life and for the opportunity to share our oft-overlooked corner of the world in such a positive and powerful way.

To Lindsey Weidhorn, thank you for being the catalyst of all this and for the creative force you'll be in Helen's life someday.

To our assistant Lindsay Miller, thank you for being our hands and feet and keeping our affairs in order when we were buried in writing and edits.

To Tim Harland, our security blanket behind the camera, thank you for being a creative mentor, ambassador of goodwill, and surrogate uncle to the world at large.

To Angie, our showrunner who sacrifices so much to make sure the days go smoothly.

To Mimi, thank you for taking care of the most important part of our lives when we have to work. Helen is lucky to have you.

To Ross and Laura, honorary framily members, thank you for taking a chance by being the first *Home Town* home. You were our first and dearest.

To Judi and Laurel Main Street, who make the things we've dreamed for our city into something real.

To Hope, thank you for the email from Manila that changed the trajectory of our lives.

To Kandace, thank you for being a friend and being kind even when our classmates were not.

To Lisa, thank you for your advice, your prayers, your example as a parent, and always reminding us to be mindful of simply "taking the next right step."